MESSAGES

'Today, when governmental surveillance and the official documentation of every aspect of existence are once again multiplying so aggressively that many people feel their core individuality to be threatened, Zweig's impassioned pursuit of personal freedom seems more relevant than ever'
Newsweek

'At a time of monetary crisis and political disorder, of mounting border controls and barbed-wire fences... Zweig's celebration of the brotherhood of peoples reminds us that there is another way'
The Nation

'Zweig takes it as a moral imperative to champion the cause of peace by reminding his readers and listeners that humanity could no longer afford the sort of belligerent nationalism that had led them into the Great War'
Inside Higher Ed

'Extraordinary and highly recommended... a lasting legacy for a new generation of readers from this memorable philosopher and dedicated historian'
Midwest Book Review

'However defeated Zweig might appear to contemporary readers, however aloof or naïve, his idea of the European soul is still worth defending... a source of insight into our troubled times'
The Northwest Review of Books

'Zweig's accumulated historical and cultural studies... remain a body of achievement almost too impressive to take in'
Clive James

STEFAN ZWEIG was born in 1881 in Vienna, a member of a wealthy Austrian-Jewish family. He studied in Berlin and Vienna and was first known as a translator and later as a biographer. Zweig travelled widely, living in Salzburg between the wars, and enjoying literary fame. His stories and novellas were collected in 1934. In the same year, with the rise of Nazism, he briefly moved to London, taking British citizenship. After a short period in New York, he settled in Brazil. It was here that he completed his acclaimed memoir *The World of Yesterday*, a lament for the golden age of a Europe destroyed by two world wars. The articles and speeches in *Messages from a Lost World* were written as Zweig, a pacifist and internationalist, witnessed this destruction and warned of the threat to his beloved Europe. On 23 February 1942, Zweig and his second wife Lotte were found dead, following an apparent double suicide. Much of his work is available from Pushkin Press.

STEFAN ZWEIG

MESSAGES FROM A LOST WORLD

Europe on the Brink

Translated from the German
by Will Stone

PUSHKIN PRESS

LONDON

Pushkin Press
71–75 Shelton Street
London, WC2H 9JQ

Original text © Atrium Press Ltd
English translation © Will Stone 2016
Foreword © John Gray 2016

First published by Pushkin Press in 2016

This edition first published in 2017

1 3 5 7 9 8 6 4 2

ISBN 978 1 782272 29 8

Designed and typeset by Tetragon, London
Printed in Great Britain by the CPI Group, UK

www.pushkinpress.com

What extraordinary changes and advances I have witnessed in my lifetime, what amazing progress in science, industry, the exploration of space, and yet hunger, racial oppression and tyranny still torment the world. We continue to act like barbarians, like savages we fear our neighbours on this earth, arm against them and they against us. I deplore to have lived at a time when man's law is to kill. The love of one's country is a natural thing but why should love stop at the border, our family is one, each of us has a duty to his brothers, we are all leaves of the same tree, and the tree is humanity...

PABLO CASALS

CONTENTS

FOREWORD BY JOHN GRAY

It is not surprising that readers are returning to the writings of Stefan Zweig. Extremely prolific and for a time extremely popular, he has suffered the neglect that often follows extraordinary literary success. The suspicion that he was overrated hung over him for many years. Yet the range and depth of his work—his arresting short stories and novellas, his vivid biographies and wide-ranging cultural commentaries, together with *The World of Yesterday*, one of the definitive twentieth-century memoirs, and *Beware of Pity*, his only full-length novel and one of the most darkly penetrating explorations of the human costs of sympathy ever written—belie this reputation. When we read Zweig now, we are rediscovering one of Europe's great writers.

The quality of Zweig's work is reason enough to return to him. But it is his quintessentially European outlook that makes him such a necessary writer today. Zweig embodied some of the central contradictions of the twentieth-century European mind. High idealism coexisted in him alongside a painful perception of the fragility of civilization. He believed passionately that Europe could cease to be a continent of squabbling nationalities and ethnicities. Yet his attachment to the old "world of security"—the liberal Hapsburg realm that he described with nostalgic fondness

in *The World of Yesterday*—prevented him from embracing
the faith that society could be reconstructed on a radically
different model. He never shared the belief—or delusion—
that a new civilization was being built in Soviet Russia. For
Zweig, a better world could only be an extension of the
world he had lost.

If Zweig did not share the faith in Communism of so
many interwar European writers and thinkers, neither
was he confident that the liberal civilization in which he
had been reared could be renewed. Zweig's professions
of idealism sound more like triumphs of the will over an
essentially pessimistic intellect than genuine affirmations
of hope, and in some ways they blinded him to the extrem-
ities of his time. Deeply attached to cosmopolitan ideals,
he failed to appreciate how these ideals were already being
challenged in *fin-de-siècle* Vienna, where a virulently anti-
Semitic mayor came to power in 1897 after several attempts
by the Emperor Franz Joseph to block the appointment had
failed. Some of the texts collected here show him struggling with the enormity of the catastrophe that followed
Europe's descent into civil war in 1914. Towards the end of
'The Tower of Babel', published in May 1916, he writes of
"the monstrous moment we are living through today". But
he was slow to respond to the threat of Nazism, seeing it
as merely an extreme manifestation of the familiar evil of
nationalism. He repeated this view in his lecture on 'The
Unification of Europe', scheduled to be given in Paris in
1934 but never delivered, and—failing even then to grasp
the unprecedented and radical evil that Nazism embodied—reiterated it again in 1941 in his speech to the New

York Pen Club, 'In This Dark Hour'. The signs of danger were clear, but—unlike Nietzsche, whose conception of a "good European" he admired and attempted to realize in himself—Zweig could not acknowledge that modern Europe harboured a deadly potential for a new type of barbarism.

It was probably only when he had decided to kill himself that Zweig really came to believe that Europe had itself (as he put it) "committed suicide". Having fled the Nazi-dominated continent where his books were being burnt, first for Britain, then America and finally Brazil, he seems to have come to the decision after hearing of the fall of Singapore. When he and his wife Lotte ended their lives on 23rd February 1942, not much more than a week after Singapore fell, it was as if he were drawing down a curtain on any possibility of a rebirth of the European civilization he loved. To the end he continued writing, finishing and sending off the manuscript of *The World of Yesterday* to his publisher only days before he ended his life. But his will to go on living had foundered.

Zweig was most European in his acute self-awareness. It is hard to read *Beware of Pity*—the story of an Austrian cavalry officer who out of compassion for a crippled girl makes her promises he cannot fulfil and which lead to her taking her own life—without thinking of Lotte, who could surely have made a future for herself if she had not been persuaded to intertwine her fate so closely with Zweig's. Her self-sacrifice was tragically unnecessary. By the time she and Zweig acted on their suicide pact, the tide of barbarism had started to turn. America joined the war in December 1941, soon after the Japanese attack on Pearl Harbor, while Soviet forces were bringing the Nazi advance into Russia to a standstill. If Zweig had hung on only a few months longer and not surrendered to panic, he would have seen that despite all the crimes that Nazism would yet perpetrate—including the supreme crime of the Holocaust—Europe's self-destruction was not yet final or complete. He and Lotte could have lived on. Instead, the potent and unstable mix of high-minded European idealism and no less European pessimism that infuses Zweig's work produced the despair that paralysed him and then killed them both.

Zweig's suspicions regarding Europe are more compelling than his insistent declarations of faith in its future. This is especially so today, when Europe seems to have reverted to an historical mean of chronic crisis. With a resurgence of nationalism in many countries and the inability of European institutions to come up with any coherent response to the migrants who are fleeing to the continent in search of safety, Zweig's hopes of European unity are remote from any realistically imaginable future. But this is what gives the texts collected here their urgent topicality. Suspended between unrealizable ideals and unmanageable realities, the self-division of Europe finds striking contemporary expression in this brilliant and self-divided writer. His doubts and fears are those of his readers, and resonate as strongly today as ever.

JOHN GRAY
October 2015

There is no doubt that the European spirit exists, but it is still in a latent state. We can be as certain about that as the astronomer who sees appear in his telescope a star whose mass has revealed to him existence. Although the European spirit may not be manifest, we know with mathematical certitude that it exists.

STEFAN ZWEIG
(From: 'Response to an enquiry on the European spirit', published in *Les Nouvelles littéraires*, 4th July 1936)

What then are the evils which weigh on humanity at this hour? What at this moment is the principal danger? Is it the excess of sangfroid, of reason, of critical acumen? Good God, no! On the contrary, it is the vertiginous development amongst the masses of these new fanaticisms, which are fascism, racism, nationalism, Communism, or the diverse strains measured out from their mix. It is the culture of exaltation as a system of government; it is official production and the procession of gratifications from scientists who conjoin old knowledge with new technological procedures. It is admiration for certain individuals driven up against the most degrading forms of idolatry. It is the savage prohibition of all critical spirit, of all exercise in lucid reason. It is an assemblage of feverishly aroused states who report from the most insanely barbaric ages and who are quite justly terrified of those spiritual worldly leaders of humanity who have safeguarded the essence of its destiny.

JULES ROMAINS
(From: *Stefan Zweig, grand Européen*, 1939)

Thanks to the pathological alienation which the nationalistic idiocy has established and still establishes among European peoples, thanks as well to the short-sighted politicians with hasty hands who are on top today with the help of this idiocy and have no sense of how the politics of disintegration which they carry on can necessarily only be politics for an intermission, thanks to all this and to some things today which are quite impossible to utter, now the most unambiguous signs that Europe wants to become a unity are being overlooked or wilfully and mendaciously reinterpreted.

FRIEDRICH NIETZSCHE
(From: *Beyond Good and Evil*, 1886)

TRANSLATOR'S
INTRODUCTION

I

In the course of his long and creatively buoyant period of
exile through the 1930s, Stefan Zweig expressed, in a slew
of speeches and articles presented in conferences across
Europe, one thing more than any other: his ardent desire
to see a unification of European states, a Europe pledged
to friendship, united around pluralism, freedom of thought
and movement, a vigorous pan-Europeanism to offset the
mounting threat of nationalism, totalitarianism and imper-
ialism. Despite the increasingly desperate situation during
the 1930s as Nazism consolidated its grip and prospects
for peace faded, Zweig kept up his utopian mantra well
beyond the point of no return, for presumably no other
reason than that it was in his view right and honourable
to do so, advancing the humanistic argument, the only
rational and dignified response in his eyes to the deranged
machinations of Nazism. But Zweig was an internation-
ally famous author, perhaps more widely read than any
other in these years; his historical biographies and fine-cut
gemstones of fiction were devoured the world over, and
people waited on his word—the Jewish community, the top

tier of European artists and writers—for it was expected of the great cosmopolitan author that forceful anti-Nazi statements would be made, denunciations of Nazi crimes, perhaps even a veiled call for a Jewish homeland. But Zweig did not deliver any of these things, visibly shrinking back from the *Realpolitik* of the hour; and this failure to weigh in publicly and visibly like other writers such as Thomas Mann, who made radio broadcasts denouncing the Nazis, was seen as indefensible by the majority of his contemporaries, casting a partial shadow over his exile and later colouring responses to his suicide.

Zweig abhorred politics, seeing it as the Antichrist to spiritual freedom, and thus distanced himself from it all his life. He saw a corrupt politics as having brought about the inferno of 1914 and the unstable aftermath. He firmly believed that he would do more harm than good to be sucked into a partisan position, even on Hitler. His pathological fear of his words being used for another's ends, of his well-intentioned statement inadvertently stoking the flames, caused an impulse to recoil from any intervention, however justified. In this calculation it can logically be argued that he was wrong, for Hitler was surely a special case of extreme evil, a civilization-destroyer who required a beyond-normal-behaviour reaction; but Zweig indentified perhaps too literally with the humanist peacemakers and tolerance-preachers of the past, such as Erasmus or Castellio, and living "counsellors" like the arch-pacifist Romain Rolland. This conviction to keep above the melee was further endorsed by his eleventh-hour reading of Montaigne, whom he found had pursued a similar solitary path, extricating himself from the feelers of the opposing factions and thereby, in Zweig's eyes, retaining his inner authenticity in an earlier time of chaos and barbarism. Yet Zweig despised Hitler and the Nazis as much as anyone and harboured a special loathing for Goebbels's insidious propaganda, which he rightly saw as the most dangerous element in Nazism's machinery of diabolism. Even as his books were tossed on the pyres and he was obliged to break with his long-standing German publishers Insel Verlag, Zweig wore his pacifist cosmopolitanism, his right to stand apart from politics, like cerebral body armour. But this was the same man whose conscience had commanded him to express his revulsion for war, his condemnation of the madness of the time, the overreaching spirit of violence and conquest in his poetic and prophetic drama *Jeremias* (1917).

Much has been said about Zweig's tendency to hang on too long in perilous situations and then make ill-starred decisions. Friderike Zweig was only too aware of her husband's difficulty in this respect, his tendency to waver until too late. When he did make a political calculation it was often deemed naive or a blunder of sorts. In his biography *European of Yesterday* (1972), Donald Prater states: "Zweig's political ideas were generally immature and ill thought out, and where he appeared to possess political insight this was often more from instinct than from clear or logical perception." This phobia of politics and resolute "apolitical" stance has its origins in the Nietzschean drive for aestheticism, which Zweig seized on, for he like Nietzsche saw the political class and materialism as the mainstays of nationalism and European spiritual decay. But it also comes from Zweig's instinctual sense that the zone of art and literature is quite apart from anything political or social, that the inward self must stay pure. This is surely why we see him drift away from Romain Rolland's influence only at the moment when the old man falls under the spell of Communism.

This ideal may seem to us repugnant when faced with the threat of Nazism, but this is simplistic, for Zweig was looking I suspect beyond his rhetorical public statement to what uncontainable tentacles would inevitably sprout from it, and he sincerely believed for better or worse that he could do more to persuade through his works, for example *Erasmus* (1934). Having said all this there is also evidence which shows that Zweig at certain moments acted boldly and decisively, even ruthlessly, his sudden departure from Salzburg being the most obvious. And in all these departures and arrivals during his intercontinental exile he behaves rationally and methodically, not to mention thoughtfully, sorting out his affairs beforehand, ensuring his manuscripts and library will serve the public good, that friends and domestic staff are well taken care of. Whilst in London, a city he claimed he loved because he was largely left to himself, Zweig worked tirelessly from his Hallam Street flat for Jewish friends and the stream of exiles who appealed to him for help with visas, connections and so forth, their constant entreaties exhausting his resources of patience and time. As always with Zweig there are curious contrasts, the interplay of conscious proaction and inaction proving a labyrinthine challenge for critics and biographers.

With the advent of Hitler, Zweig was initially drawn into the radicalizing potential of the National Socialists, before leaping out as it were from a burning building. Zweig thought this new movement, though evidently repulsive, might stir things up, liberate the middle classes and offset what he saw as the infection of bourgeois materialism menacing the treasured spirit of France in particular. Zweig adored France above all other nations and unsurprisingly viewed her as the natural cradle of the arts and civilized intellectual activity, the model of his civilized Europe of the spirit. He like others presumed Hitler was a transitory phenomenon, an aberration, a spark of extremism which might have beneficial side effects before being summarily extinguished. Although this delusion was short-lived, as was his episode of Germanic pride at the outset of the First World War (discussed later), it appears to reinforce what Prater claims regarding Zweig's slowness to realize the course of events at the beginning of momentous political change. But conversely it may also explain why Zweig corrected himself by later abandoning his Salzburg home so suddenly and thoroughly. Zweig might have been slow to see the light, but once his eyes were opened he acted without deliberation.

Zweig's spiritual internationalist outlook was really based on a long-developed and honed network of culturally enriching relationships across central Europe, or as Prater has it, "Zweig was quietist, seeing in internationalism not a political programme, but the sum of personal connections forged through friendship." His vision was to extend his own model, to upgrade the most valuable element of the lost "golden age" before the First World War when these friendships were formed, both to act as a foil to the pernicious and ever more unstable reality represented by totalitarianism, and to provide a design for a future European situation beyond that of the present, whose survival he severely doubted. Zweig's inherent idealism, his overriding passion for establishing a creatively ennobling society of nations, was underwritten by periods of striking artistic achievement in the past, most notably the Renaissance. At first sight all this may appear to us today laudable, naturally desirable, yet surely grossly out of touch with the bestial realities taking place on the ground, amongst peoples cut off from Zweig's privileged elite. His determination to imagine Europe as a kind of spiritual engine house for the next key stage in mankind's ascension appears now, in our present age of commonplace violent extremism and materialist decadence, as out of time as it did then, at the moment when Hitler, engorged with imperial fantasies, swept his hand impatiently back and forth across the map table in Berchtesgaden. However, the sheer passion and belief, the intelligence, the evident richness of learning, the valuable sediment as it were of a lifetime's thought and reflection Zweig conjures in support of his dream remains valid and curiously seductive. Whatever the retorts, this is no vague chimera.

II

In the pieces collected here, Stefan Zweig strives to bring his European ideal down from the clouds and place it on terra firma; for example, in places he argues robustly for progressive education, in order to change deep-seated attitudes on race and Fatherland and encourage a new fluidity of thought, the interweaving of languages and cultures. The reader will soon see that these essays themselves interlink and one is merely reinforcing another; though the outlying theme may be different the central message remains the same. Nationalism is the sworn enemy of civilization, whether past, present or future, its malodorous presence thwarting the development of intelligence, its tenets those of division, regression, hatred, violence and persecution. In nationalism, with the Nazis as its most lethal form, Zweig sees the agent which may finally destroy his European heartlands, finishing the job the First World War started. Zweig's Europe is an almost mystical conviction that whatever remains of the European spirit, the sum of artistic achievement that has accrued for centuries, can only survive the modern plague of nationalism, materialism and philistinism, can only safeguard its crown jewels of philosophical thought, art and literature through a practicable spiritual integration, a higher guild of amiable coalition. What Zweig proposes is a moral defence of the European soul against the very same forces which menace our Europe now in 2015, sanity against insanity, unity against division, tolerance against intolerance, intelligence against ignorance.

But what of this spiritual unity? Is it just another word for pan-Europeanism, such as the mobile professional elites enjoy in the privileged strata of a technologically unified Europe today, or a rhetorical comfort blanket for those who see their national language and traditions dying on the world stage (notably the French, who habitually accord Zweig mythical proportions), or is there any substance to it? In these disparate pieces, culled from declarative pauses during his wanderings in exile, Zweig argues forcefully that there is. Moving and haunting, especially with the gift of hindsight, inherently tragic when planted before the brush fire of bestial realities sweeping across the continent as he wrote, yet paradoxically also morally persuasive, these pieces show Zweig repeatedly setting out his manifesto for cultural health through fraternity in the face of a Europe gradually slipping away into fanaticism, apathy, political expediency and the spectre of genocidal terror. Whether delivering a lecture in Rome or Zurich, in London or Paris, whether attending yet another conference in the ever-shrinking free-thinking world, humanistic symposiums whose influence on events he knew only too well were depressingly limited, Zweig is urgently reiterating the need for change, for action not more words. Yet in the unstable climate of imperialist muscle-flexing and virulent propaganda during the 1930s, the action required, the necessary turnaround, which he espouses so earnestly in his speeches, is held in check by the sheer physical and psychological power of the extremist forces which are already unleashed.

Since the present appears hopeless, Zweig looks to the future and the generation beyond his own, the survivors, like himself after the First World War, speaking to an audience both within and crucially beyond the present calamity. Of course that future did herald an eventual Franco-German dream collective of European nation states, and out of this techno-bureaucratic conglomeration one could argue that something of Zweig's dream has become a reality, namely in the successful European exchange of culture,

sport and the arts. But Zweig's exultant vision of fraternity under one continental roof has hardly been realized,
since nation states have in spite of the past clung on to
their self-serving national powers and their nationalist
arrogance with tenacity. In the extraordinary, recently
discovered text 'The Unification of Europe: A Discourse',
a speech prepared to be given in Paris in 1934 but then
mothballed, Zweig puts forward the novel idea of a "capital
city of Europe" whose location would change each year,
giving each country a chance to be master of the greater
union. Today's policy of "European capital of culture" is
something Zweig would have certainly applauded, but it
is really attractive window-dressing. The sad truth is that
Zweig's noble premise of nations purged of animosity
towards one another, intellectually advancing in interlingual
creativity, could only happen, then as today, *if* the people
of Europe really wanted it to happen. But through the progressive decades of the 1960s, 1970s and 1980s, behind the
self-congratulatory fanfares and chatter of policy-making
from Brussels, nationalism lurked in one gruesome form
or another, apparently muzzled on the fringes, kept at bay
from the great project. Now, as fanatical Islam extends
its grip and correspondingly Islamophobia rises, as the
union stutters and stalls in monetary crisis, the far right
is emboldened as never before, has slipped its chains, and
we watch helpless as it sends out its hideous spawn. Zweig
and the later constructors of the union all overlooked or
optimistically sidelined a disturbing fact: that people might
sign up to a collective if it does not disadvantage them,
primarily in economic terms, but all the same they have

the door to the motherland left ajar, ready to leap through it with the national flag whenever the time is right. The union does not replace the old enmities, the old fault lines. In their rush to renovate the European house, the decorators of the union merely laid consecutive layers of fresh wallpaper over a mouldy wall, and now those living in the house see the mould showing through again. Zweig's grand European hothouse of the soul, a microclimate where hostility is an anachronism, did not come to pass, nor—let us be candid—did Zweig probably expect it to; but for us today, these ardent "lost messages", in their endorsement of a stillborn yet still possible future, surely hold a special relevance, for they have been found, translated and made available to anglophone readers at a precarious moment for Western civilization, as to Europe's outer walls the outriders of atrocity are gathering.

III

In May 1916, at the dark heart of the First World War, Zweig's brief essay 'The Tower of Babel' was simultaneously published in the warring countries of France and Germany. Zweig employs the ancient myth of the doomed tower, more as an attractive template than as an effective analogy, for the grave situation in which the stricken vessel Europe presently found itself, holed and rudderless in an ocean of unprecedented ruin and dislocation following the storm surge of nationalism unleashed by war. The Babel essay appeared in the April/May edition of the Geneva-based journal *Le Carmel*, supported by Romain Rolland,

and on 8th May 'Der Turm zu Babel' was published in the *Vossische Zeitung* in Berlin. As is well known, the Tower of Babel myth concerns mankind's attempt, through communal ambition and spiritual accord, to build a tower high enough to reach heaven; it is spotted by God and humanity is summarily punished with eternal disunity for its excess of pride. The workers of all nations abandon their labours half finished and return for good to their individual lands, to reside in new-found insularity and suspicion. The half-completed tower falls into melancholy decay. Zweig enters at this point, transforming the tower into a symbol of Europe's destiny, urging the workers (the European nations) who have downed tools and fled into their relevant clans to return to the construction site and continue work on the noble edifice they started and which, because of their desertion, is now a ruin. Zweig's premise is simple: that humanity is capable of achieving unimaginable heights when it works together, pooling its creative resources and individual strengths in a common ambition, but conversely will achieve nothing, become degraded and eventually self-destruct when it is split into rival communities, each believing it is superior to another. It is a way out of this depressing cycle, this human impasse, that Zweig probes in these texts, highlighting history and artistic creativity as our most instructive guides.

Into the 1920s, with the war still fresh in their minds, Zweig and his "Good European" brethren believed that if Europe was to save itself from a further even more unimaginable catastrophe, a spiritual renaissance in Europe must be sought. The brutal shock of the war, the attendant protracted freezing of borders and physical impossibility of travel, the unimaginable casualties had rudely interrupted this boon of fluid cultural exchange. Whilst the roaming poet Walt Whitman sang of the pre-eminence of the continent of America, a piqued Émile Verhaeren, generally viewed as his Old World equivalent, retorted with insistence on the continued pre-eminence of the old European one. But Verhaeren, one of the elder statesman of Europe's writerly elite, whom Zweig revered as a quasi-prophet of the new age, was fatally crushed by a train in Rouen station six months after Zweig published his Babel essay. Zweig, whose close relationship to Verhaeren was nevertheless eroded by the war, was hemmed in by closed borders and could not attend the funeral. Each had been stuck in his own land for the duration and there, to a lesser or greater extent, was infected initially by national pride. All were caught up in the event and few were immune from this scourge, at least initially. Zweig himself was guilty: his passions aroused, he enthusiastically logged the German army's first triumphs. Even the scrupulously judicious Rilke penned ill-starred lines he later renounced, but worst of all the pro-European elder they all looked to, Verhaeren, had succumbed, penning *La Belgique sanglante* (*Belgium Bleeding*, 1915), scabrous, unbridled criticisms of German culture following massacres by German troops in Flanders, before eventually coming to his senses. These aberrations on the part of ordinarily deep-thinking, sensitive, peaceable writers and poets reveal to us just how radical and disorientating the course of events was, how the abrupt breaching of the dam of peace caused a deluge of virulent mutual accusation and national self-justification even amongst those supposedly immune from it. However, only two months into the war Zweig was already writing the poetic prose of 'The Sleepless World', the piece which opens this collection, a haunting, almost hallucinatory vision of the perpetual state of watchfulness, anxiety and confusion war induces in all sentient beings it touches. "Each became gradually enmeshed in the great event; no one could remain cool in the fiery delirium of the world. Constancy is helpless when realities are utterly transformed, none could stand aloof, secure on his rock above the waves, looking down and smiling knowingly at a world wracked with fever. Whether aware of what was happening or not, all were borne on the current, with no idea where it was leading." It is, then, these four years of trauma, of horror, isolation and landlocked frustration, the melancholy procession of those reluctant coffin-bearers of the "golden age" that languished up to the summer of 1914, which form the crucible to Zweig's fervent appeals for a united Europe two decades later. The loss of that pre-war Europe dogged Zweig until the moment he bowed out in Petrópolis, Brazil. He was in effect a man carrying a sickness which he could never recover from and for which in any case there was no cure.

Interestingly, 'The Tower of Babel' enjoyed a resurrection when it was republished in the Budapest-based German-language paper *Pester Lloyd* on the auspicious date of 1st January 1930. Incredibly, on the very first day of a new decade, which will usher in the most devastating series of events ever to blight humanity, Zweig is there with his call for reconstruction. And Zweig revisits the myth again two years later in the essay 'European Thought in its Historical Development', given at a conference in Florence on 5th May 1932. With Hitler warming up for his election triumph the following year, Europe's alternative construction foreman Zweig is busy handing out spades and picks. "This myth taken from the opening pages of the Bible is a wonderful symbol that with humanity as a community all is possible, even the highest aspirations, but only when it is united, and never when it is partitioned into languages and nations which do not understand each other and do not want to understand each other. And perhaps—who knows what mysterious memories can still be traced in our blood—there is still some vague reminiscence in our spirit of those distant times, the Platonic memory of when humanity was united and the persuasive, haunted longing that it might eventually recommence the unfinished work; in any case, this dream of a unified world, a unified humanity, is more ancient than all literature, art and scientific knowledge." With almost a seer's conviction, Zweig sees the answer to today's disintegrating Europe in terms of the re-emergence of deep longings and dreams actively realized in a distant past. Rather unhelpfully sounding like some ironic inversion of Nazi blood theories, Zweig believes that the potential for spiritual development is buried deep within each of us: having been secreted in the blood of our ancestors, it passes down to us through the ages and through enlightenment and education it can be restored, however barbaric the epoch in which we reside. Only then can the half-finished work be completed, only then can the tower rise to its intended heights.

IV

The texts gathered in this collection are all stamped with the same hallmark, a stark question which underpins all other concerns for Zweig in these years. The question is this. After the unparalleled disaster of the First World War, will Europe once again transform itself into a battlefield, but this time destroy itself completely? This is the question Zweig carries with him out of the aftermath of the First World War through to the moment he leaves his Salzburg house for exile in London in 1934 and which is finally laid to rest in Petrópolis in February 1942. As the years pass the question becomes ever more onerous to bear. It is futile to ponder the moral intricacies of Zweig's suicide in Brazil in 1942 without taking into account the veiled anguish revealed in these essays. The reason Zweig ended his life was essentially that the question of Europe's destruction had for him been definitively answered. Isolated in Brazil, he became convinced that the Europe he had dedicated his writing life to had now destroyed itself, if not quite yet physically then spiritually. Zweig sensed that whatever was left of Europe after Nazism's fires had burnt themselves out would be unable to resurrect itself as it had in the past following episodes of barbarism. The last chance of the inter-war years would not be replayed. The great project of civilization, as Zweig saw it, which had been evolving for three millennia, the central artery to his creative life, the very essence of his being, had been so retarded by Hitler's radical evil that whatever came afterwards would be either hopelessly corrupted or, worse, a deceiving doppelgänger, a facade.

Perhaps Zweig thought back to Nieuwpoort and Diksmuide, the shell-pulverized villages of Flanders, to Ypres, which he witnessed after the war, shocked at these "dummy" villages and towns, which were exact replicas but lacked any soul. This absence of soul, the possible eradication of the sense of meaning which accrues from the passage of human time, that is, everything "old Europe" represented, must have caused Zweig the most grievous suffering.

However, what these pieces show us is how deeply Zweig, who was at various moments morbidly depressed, still believed in this seemingly hopeless humanity's potential for change, the chance of renewed ascension. So even while his books were being tossed on pyres on the Domplatz in Salzburg, his house invaded by police, his right to publish in Germany ended, he could still turn to History, "that poetess", and see hopeful parallels, how after each impossibly dark stage of history a new light had irresistibly dawned. Even as late as 1938/39, as the borders of Europe thicken with troops and tanks, Zweig is at pains to communicate his ideal as something other than an ideal, to make it appear feasible through concrete examples, however tenuous some may be in practical terms. In order to react meaningfully against the irresistible morbid flow of events, Zweig realizes that words are futile and yet that is all he has. It is this melancholic realization that the implicitly violent and "revolutionary" new age delivered by Hitler has by its very inception and presence moved far beyond the existing parameters, the awareness that the course of destruction is already set that exhausts Zweig. But doggedly he continues his quest because it is the humane one, the right one, the

only path which morally guarantees him a purity of intent
and a legacy of decency in the face of depravity. In short,
it is the only path which allows him to go on living in a
world he feels is intolerable. He repeats his message, and
the message remains fundamentally the same whether it
is 1916, 1932 or 1940.

It should be remembered, as Jules Romains points out
in *Stefan Zweig: grand Européen* (1939), that the largest part
of Zweig's published writing is in the domain of the essay
form. Beyond the espousal of a European ideal, the essays
here not only display some of Zweig's greatest attributes
as a writer, but also reveal crucial elements of biography
which serve as foundations for or addenda to *The World
of Yesterday* (1942). This is most clearly the case in the
essays 'The Historiography of Tomorrow' and 'European
Thought in Its Historical Development', and most vividly
in the haunting and elegiac 'The Vienna of Yesterday',
which Zweig presented at the Théâtre Marigny on his
last visit to Paris in April 1940. The genuine affection of
Zweig for his home city is here laid bare and the period of
Vienna's impoverishment after the 1918 armistice vividly
and insightfully portrayed. Zweig manages to capture the
peculiar atmosphere of the once grand and opulent city
reduced to decrepitude, but still remaining proud, through
a series of impressionistic flourishes that convince. Music,
Zweig reveals to us, as he does elsewhere in these pieces,
is the real lifeblood of humanity, and in this case of the
old Hapsburg capital. It is also perhaps its saviour. The
account of a concert by Vienna's finest musicians held
in an unheated auditorium with an audience of citizen

paupers dressed in threadbare coats is to be treasured. The essay closes with a poignantly understated line whose polite vagueness, by veiling the horrific reality, paradoxically emphasizes it: "Of today's Vienna I can say nothing. We know very little of what is happening there, we are even fearful of interpreting it too exactly."

In the essay 'History as Poetess' (1931), Zweig shows the central position of history in his world view and in his writings. He paints history not as the mere roll call of facts and dates, but as "the workshop of God", where facts are only made meaningful by the poetic authority of those who transmit them. Once more, the notion of a European or world community saturates the text: "history only lives where it achieves a certain poetic grandeur, which is why the highest accomplishment of a people is to transform as much of its *national* history into *world* history as possible, its private people's myth into a world myth". He also says: "A nation gains more power in the spiritual space, the more poetically it can present its historical existence and development in the world." Zweig lambasts the "ersatz" history of popular romantic biography favoured in the present, castigating those who muddle historical fact and adjust it to suit their story and in order to sell more copies. Zweig praises the genuine creative storytellers, those who take the raw material of historical fact and, without adulterating it, place it before us in such a way that it becomes meaningful, enhancing our knowledge rather than leaving us with a falsified theatrical approximation.

'The Historiography of Tomorrow' (1939) begins with the portrait of Europe being locked in a moral crisis and its peoples the victims of a persistent angst, all a by-product of world war. Like a doctor searching for a cure whilst his patient ebbs away on the operating table, Zweig determines that the artificially feverish atmosphere, like any drug or stimulant prescribed for too long, must be reduced. Zweig has noted how when the war, and thus "the obligatory hatred and murder", abruptly ends, "like turning off a gas tap", it cannot be expected that the populace will relinquish the impulses they have become accustomed to over four years. Thus the so-called peace is anything but. Zweig argues that the militaristic generation which inflicted this nightmare on mankind must be shed like a rotten branch, allowing new progressive branches to grow from the European trunk. For this there must be a wholly new conception of history, with a spiritual bent, focusing on intellectual and scientific achievements rather than military prowess and flag-waving heroism. He criticizes the way history was taught in his own youth, always reinforcing a nationalistic outlook, where each country feels that it alone must be the most powerful, the most righteous one. Zweig thunders, "With our blood seething in our veins, we can only tremble at the thought that, due to this kind of skewed education, the innocent and credulous new generation of young people might be heading for an even more appalling bloodbath than the last." Only by introducing a new vision of history as the holding pen of the creative spirit will mankind recover from this "fever", this bacillus, and extricate itself from the cycle of destruction. "It is only in this way that we can console ourselves and guard against the insanity of nationalism and dictators who are bent on launching peoples against one another, ever forcing us backwards politically when the natural momentum is to go forwards. Only when we access this new sense of being will we learn the history of tomorrow; only then will it be possible no longer to despair at our epoch and to retain, even if we failed as citizens, the pride to be men of our time. Only then will we be able to face without horror the bloody vortex of history, when we see it as a necessary creative stage for a new and more meaningful future, as preparation for a complete reworking of humanity."

v

One of Zweig's preoccupations, which appears in a number of his essays, is the stark difference between the atmosphere preceding the conflict in 1914 and that in 1939 and its repercussions for Europe. In the fascinating comparison essay '1914 and Today' (1936), Zweig sees his generation as being blind to events, craftily hoodwinked, deceived into war by a minority of determined warmongers who took advantage of the naivety and trustfulness of the people who, on the eve of conflict, still believed at the eleventh hour that it could never happen, and that all was being done to prevent it, that the great socialist leaders would never let it happen, when in fact, due to the machinations of a clutch of powerfully positioned, unscrupulous individuals and the irresistible tide of fate, it had already begun. But in 1939/40 we see the polar opposite. "Whilst in 1914 every intellectual, every politician dared not speak of war or seem to glorify it, today in Europe and in Japan whole peoples are educated and

disciplined solely with a view to waging war and with blatant cynicism the whole economic structure of the country
is galvanized with this single aim in mind." Zweig repeats
this theme in a later essay, 'Gardens in Wartime' (Stefan
Zweig, *Journeys*, Hesperus Press, 2010), which he wrote in
England in 1940, while he experienced the so-called phoney
war. Comparing it with the febrile gung-ho atmosphere of
1914, he explains that "in 1939 war did not arise suddenly,
it simply gave concrete forms to fears already present…
they endured the war because it was necessary to do so,
as something inevitable." Here, in the 1936 essay, this idea
has already formed. "They await war as if for a perfectly
natural event, almost as if of necessity, and that is why the
current generation has no excuse to be 'surprised' by war
as in 1914. For it is laboriously announced, prepared quite
openly and lucidly. It is not only at the door, it already has
its foot in the house."

Zweig's attempt to go behind the scenes of the artistic
process, 'The Secret of Artistic Creation' (1938), consists
of his long-gestated musings on the mysterious processes
leading to a finished work. This was a subject which Zweig,
experienced collector of manuscripts, musical scores and
autographs, not to mention psychological profiler of great
artistic and historical figures, would have been particularly
drawn to. Rather cleverly Zweig compares investigating
this phenomenon to elements of criminology. Although
he admits we can never truly know the interior process
and should not wish to, we can up to a point "retroactively
reconstruct it". This essay is a tour de force of reflection on
the laborious trials or relative ease of the creative process,

how each masterpiece is formed at greatly differing speeds and through starkly contrasting processes, according to the habits, vagaries and natural creative velocity of the artist. Zweig, with his immense archive of sources, draws on a range of examples, notably in music, comparing Mozart and Beethoven, Haydn and Wagner, and so on. Zweig concludes: "To create is a constant struggle between the unconscious and the conscious. Without these two elements the creative act cannot happen. They constitute the indispensable foundation; it is within the law of contrast, the final compromise between conscious and unconscious that the artist is imprisoned. Within the limits of this law he remains free."

The collection closes with 'In This Dark Hour', one of Zweig's final addresses, a touching speech made to the Pen Club in New York, 1941, heavy with portent and yet displaying characteristic eloquent resistance. Here, Zweig broaches the subject of being a writer in German at a time of acute German shame, stating how he welcomes the fact that he and others have been rejected by "those who have plunged this world into the greatest catastrophe in all history", but how the burden of being an accessory to their crimes by dint of origin weighs heavy: "we must bear these violations as a secret and odious shame." Zweig confesses that he cannot abandon the German language, despite the poison with which it is now infected, for, true to form, he argues that it was the language in which "we fought against the self-glorification of nationalism". Zweig, though, does not, as Thomas Mann did, conveniently distinguish between a Germany of Nazis and a free Germany;

Zweig sees Germany as guilty one and all. He has rejected Germany, the country he was closest to, where he was published and admired, yet this rejection was a long time coming and painfully borne. In divers letters to Joseph Roth we see this struggle, as Roth constantly beseeches Zweig to loose the mooring.

Zweig's last hope is that the supreme evil of Hitler and his cohorts has inadvertently given rise to a reactive surge for a renewed sense of liberty and inner strength. "It was necessary for this dark hour to fall, perhaps the darkest in history, to make us realize that freedom is as vital to our soul as breathing to our body. I know—never has the dignity of man been so abased as now, nor peoples so enslaved and maltreated; never has the divine image of the Creator in all His forms been so vilely defiled and martyred—but never, my friends, never ever has humanity been more aware than now that freedom is indispensable to the soul." These essays in a sense announce the spiritual will and testament of Stefan Zweig, serving as lucid and expressive declarations of his inner conviction. Though, due to the perennial human aptitude for stupidity and folly, we might not yet be in a position to execute them, even entertain their plausibility, and perhaps never will, we can at least respect the intellectual knowingness and openness with which they are imbued, the insatiable curiosity and sagacity they display, the personal courage they exhibit—a powerful statement of one man's belief in the potential of humanity to regenerate and compensate for its most heinous crimes.

WILL STONE
October 2015

THE SLEEPLESS
WORLD

THERE IS LESS SLEEP in the world today; longer are the nights and longer the days. In each land of this limitless Europe, in every city, every street, every house, every apartment, the reposeful breath of sleep is now clipped and feverish; like an oppressive and stifling summer night, this inferno of an epoch glows over us, throwing the senses into confusion. Numberless are those who, on whichever side, would otherwise drift through the nocturnal hours in the dark skiff of sleep—gilded with colourful and gently fluttering dreams—but nightly now hear the clocks march, march, march along the hellish path from daylight to daylight, enduring the burrowing beetle of anxieties and dark thoughts relentlessly gnawing and devouring, until the heart is left raw and ailing. From now on all humanity is in thrall to this fever both night and day, a state of terrible and all-consuming watchfulness, sending its shower of sparks across the heightened senses of millions, fate entering, invisibly, by thousands of windows and doors, chasing out sleep, chasing forgetfulness from every couch. There is less sleep in the world today; longer are the nights and longer the days.

Today no one can be alone with himself and his destiny, each peers out furtively into the far distance. At night, at the hour when he lies awake in his safely locked, guarded house, thoughts turn to friends and those far away: perhaps, at the same hour, a measure of his destiny is fulfilled, a cavalry charge in a Galician village, a naval attack, everything that has happened at every second across thousands and thousands of miles, all that relates to his one single life. And the soul knows, she extends and feels the intimation of a yearning to grasp it all, the burning air of all those desires and prayers, which wing back and forth from one side of the world to the other. A thousand thoughts restlessly on the move, from the silent towns to the military campfires, from the lone sentry on his watch and back again, from the nearest to the most distant, those invisible gliding threads of love and tribulation, a weft of feelings, a limitless network now covering the world, for all days and all nights. How many words they whisper now, how many prayers they send up into the indifferent ether, how much lucid love pulses through each hour of the night! Unremittingly the air quivers with secret waves for which science has no name and whose amplitude no seismograph can measure: but who can judge if they are futile, these desires, if this colossal will, burning from the depths of the soul, can overshoot distances like the vibrations of sound or the convulsions of electricity? Where there was once sleep, unsubstantial rest, there is now a desire for images: always the soul struggles to perceive through the dark night those beings far away, those held close to the heart, and via the imagination each now lives with a range of destinies. A thousand thoughts burrow into sleep, ever and again its swaying edifice topples and the image-rich darkness inclines vacantly over the solitary. Watchers of the nights, men are now also watchers of the days: at this hour, in the most ordinary people one encounters, lies living proof of the power of the orator, the poet, the prophet, for what is most secret in man is, through the diabolical pressure of daily events, forced to the exterior, so that each individual experiences a sudden burgeoning of his vitality. In the same way as elsewhere, in the exterior world, on the field of battle, plain peasants who have spent a lifetime calmly tilling their land in silence and peace are suddenly seized at the emotive hour by the heroic, and some visionary force rises like a lithe flame in people ordinarily taciturn and prone to grumbling; each and every one steps outside the communal circle of existence; those normally only concerned with the working day now sense in every message inspired reality and a compelling image. Today the people endlessly haul their plough of anxieties and visions across the barren soil of night, and, when they finally sink into sleep, surrender themselves to outlandish dreams. Then the blood runs hotter in their veins, and in this sultriness bloom tropical plants of horrors and nervousness, the dreams come, and one's only salvation is to wake and shrug them off as nothing but useless nightmares, the appalling realities of mankind's most terrible truth: the war of everyone against everyone.

Even the most peace-loving today dream of battles, columns rising for the assault and rushing across sleep, the dark blood roaring in the reverberation of the cannon. And if you suddenly awake terror-stricken you hear, with eyes wide open, the thunder of the wagons, the clatter of boots. You listen, lean from the window: and yes it's true, they're coming now in long procession, carts and horses along the deserted streets. Some soldiers lead a troop of horses by the reins, steeds that trot obediently with their heavy, deafening tread on the echoing cobbles. And they too, who normally would be resting through the night from their labours in their warm stables, these placid teams are forced apart, their benign brotherhood broken. In the stations you hear cows bellow from the cattle trucks; these patient beasts, wrenched from the warm, soft summer pastures and led into the unknown, even for them in their stupor, sleep is troubled. And the trains force a path through slumbering Nature: she too is startled by the clamour of humanity; flocks of riders gallop at night over fields which for eternity had rested peacefully in the darkness, and above the black expanse of the sea the light pools of the searchlights gleam in a thousand places, brighter than moonlight and more dazzling than the sun, while even below the darkness of the waters is disturbed by submariners seeking their prey. Shots ring out across the mountains, echoing, chasing the birds from their nests, no sleep can be assured, and even the ether, that eternally pristine space, is streaked with the murderous velocity of the aeroplane, those ill-omened comets of our time. Nothing, nothing can bring calm or rest in these days; humanity has dragged animals and nature into its murderous struggle. There is less sleep in the world today; longer are the nights and longer the days.

But let us reflect, over and again, on the vastness of time and the fact that what is occurring now has no equal in history, reflect on what it means to be only awake, unceasingly awake. Never since it came into being has

44

the whole world been so communally seized by nervous energy. Until now a war was only an isolated flare-up in the immense organism that is humanity, a suppurating limb which could be cauterized and thus healed, whilst all the remaining limbs were free to perform their normal functions without the least hindrance. There were always places that remained untouched, villages which no message from the restless activity ever reached, villages which calmly continued to divide their life between day and night, between labour and rest. Somewhere there was still sleep and silence, people who awoke at daybreak amidst gentle laughter and whose sleep was untrammelled by disturbing dreams. But due to its steady conquest of the globe, humanity forged ever-closer links, so today a fever quivers within its whole organism; horrors easily traverse the entire cosmos. There is not a workshop, not an isolated farm, not a hamlet deep in a forest from which they have not torn a man so that he might launch himself into the fray, and each of these beings is intimately connected to others by myriad threads of feeling; even the most insignificant among them has breathed so much of the feverish heat, his sudden disappearance makes those that remain that much colder, more alone and empty. Each fate leads inexorably to another fate, little circles which grow and expand in the vast sea of feeling; in this profound connection, in this mutual reinforcement of experience, no one goes into his death as into a vacuum, each takes something from others along with him. Each is pierced through by the gaze of those behind him, and this constant looking and seeing, magnified millionfold and woven into the destiny of whole nations, has created the world's current state of nervous agitation. All humanity listens keenly, and through the miracle of technology even responds at the same moment. Ships transmit messages across boundless waves, whilst the radio transmitters of Nauen and Paris fire off a message in minutes to the West African colonies and the shores of Lake Chad, as at the same moment the Indians receive it on their scrolls of hemp and lace, then the Chinese on their silk, and so on to the farthest reaches of humanity, the same feverish anxiety arrives and stifles the peaceable course of life. Each keeps watch, each remains at the open window of his senses to receive the slightest message, swallowing reassuringly the word of the heroes and dreading the doubts of the despairing. Prophets, both the genuine and the false, have assumed power over the masses, who now obey and obey again, advancing resolutely into the fever, day and night, the interminably long days and nights of this epoch which demands that each remain in perpetual wakefulness.

These days had scant respect for those who stood apart, and even those remotest from the battlefield could not disengage from it. Without exception our lives were shaken to the core, and no one, whoever he was, had the right to unmolested sleep in this monstrous excess of agitation. We were all dragged through this enforced migration of nations and peoples, which we either affirmed or denied according to our will. Each became gradually enmeshed in the great event; no one could remain cool in the fiery delirium of the world. Constancy is helpless when realities are utterly transformed; none could stand aloof, secure on his rock above the waves, looking down and smiling knowingly at a world wracked with fever. Whether aware of what was happening or not, all were borne on the current, with no idea where it was leading. No one could cut himself adrift, for our blood and spirit made us part of the river of the nation and each quickening of the current merely drew us farther on, each change in the pulse disrupted further the rhythm of our own life. What new values will exist when this fever has finally dissipated and all that appeared to remain the same will be so entirely different? The German cities, what feelings will they experience when they reflect on themselves after the war? And how different and strange will Paris seem to our new sensitivity! I know myself that from now on, in Liège say, in the same old guest house, I shall hardly be in a position to sit alongside my European friends indulging in the usual sentiments now that a load of German bombs has rained down on the citadel; for between so many friends, from whichever side of the conflict, the shadows of the fallen will be stood and their icy breath will kill any warmth of the spoken word. We will all need to relearn how to proceed from yesterday to tomorrow by way of this indecipherable today, whose violence we only perceive through still more horror, learn how to heal ourselves by finding a new structure of life beyond this ferment which turns our days white-hot and makes our nights so stiflingly oppressive. Another generation are rising undaunted behind us whose feelings have been emboldened by this inferno; they will be quite different, those who saw victories in these years where we only saw retreats, hesitation and lassitude. The pandemonium of these times will give rise to a new order, and our primary concern must be to assist in vigorously shaping it for the better.

A new order—for the sleepless fever, the restlessness, the hope and the waiting, which now consume the repose of our days and nights, surely cannot last. Even though mass destruction appears omnipresent today, monstrously spreading across a terrorized world, it is in the end nothing compared to the more powerful energy of life, which, after each interval of anguish, instills a period of recovery to ensure existence becomes stronger and still more beautiful. A new peace—oh how its light wings seem so distant today, beating through the dust and gun smoke!—will one day return and reconstruct the old order of life, labour in the day and rest at night; in thousands of living rooms now on permanent watch, in a state of nervousness and anxiety, silence will return at the moment of restful sleep regained and the stars, reassured, will once more rest their gaze on a Nature breathing easefully and returned to a state of contentment. What now wears the mask of horror already conceals the grandeur of a noble transformation; with regret and almost with a certain wistfulness we will recall those interminable nights when, through some miraculous transformation in our self, we sensed a new destiny forming in our blood and time's warm breath upon our waking lids. Only he who has lived through sickness knows the joy of the man in good health, only the insomniac knows the relief of sleep regained. Those who have returned and those who have stayed behind will be more content with life than those who have passed on: they will be able to weigh its true value and inherent beauty more precisely and accurately, and we might almost talk of a sense of anticipation for the new order, were it not for the fact that today, as in ancient times, the tiles of the temple of peace are splashed with sacrificial blood and this new blessed sleep of the world has only been bought with the death of millions of its noblest creations.

THE TOWER
OF BABEL

THE MOST ANCIENT legends of humanity tend to be inspired by our earliest origins. The symbols of these origins harbour a wonderful poetic force, announcing as they do the great moments of a later history in which peoples renew themselves and the most significant epochs have their roots. In the books of the Bible, from the very opening pages, just after the chaos of creation, one of the most impressive myths of humanity is told. In that time, only just emerging from the unknown, still enveloped by the dark shadows of the unconscious, men were brought together by a communal work. They found themselves in a foreign place, with no means of escape, a place that seemed to them uncertain and filled with dangers, but high above them they saw the sky, clear and pure, eternal mirror of the infinite, and a yearning was born in them. So they came together and said: "Come, let us build a city and a tower whose summit will reach the sky so that our name will remain for all eternity." And they joined forces, moulded the clay and fired the bricks and began to construct a tower which would extend to the domain of God above, his stars and the pale shell of the moon.

From on high God saw their puny efforts and smiled, perhaps imagining that these men of such small stature, like tiny insects, were forming still smaller things from moulded earth and sculpted stone. Below him these men were rising to the task, driven on by their desire for eternity, yet to him it seemed but an innocent game devoid of danger. But soon he saw the foundations of their tower begin to grow, because these men were united and in accord, because they never paused in their work and came to each other's assistance in a spirit of mutual harmony. So he said to himself: "They will never let that tower alone until they have finished it." For the first time he saw the greatness of the spirit which he had bestowed on men. But it dawned on him that this was not like his own spirit, which rested after seven days of labour, but quite another, both impressive and dangerous, with an indefatigable fervour which would never cease until the work was realized. And for the first time God became fearful that these men might become like him, a unity. So he began pondering ways he might slow down their labour and he knew there was nothing more effective to break their unity than sowing discord amongst them. He said to himself: "I shall disrupt them by ensuring they do not understand each other's languages." And for the first time God showed his cruelty towards mankind.

And God's dark resolution was made. He directed his hand against the men who down below worked in a spirit of unity and dedication, and smote that spirit. The bitterest hour of humanity had come. Suddenly, overnight, in the midst of their labours, men could no longer understand each other. They cried out, but had no concept of each other's speech, and so they became enraged with each other. They threw down their bricks, picks and trowels, they argued and quarrelled until finally they abandoned the communal work, each returning to his own home in his own land. They dispersed into the fields and forests of the earth and there each built his own house which did not reach the clouds, nor God, but merely sheltered his own head and his nightly slumber. The Tower of Babel, that colossal edifice, remained abandoned; the wind and rain gradually tore away the parapets, which were already approaching the sky, and little by little the whole structure crumbled away, subsided and was laid to ruin. Soon it was just a legend that appeared in the canticles and humanity completely forgot the monumental work of its youth.

Centuries and millennia passed and men lived in the isolation of their languages. They erected boundaries between their fields and territories, between their customs and beliefs, and when they crossed them it was only in order to rob. For centuries and millennia there was no unity amongst them, only their own pride, and egocentric works prospered. However, of their communal youth some vestige remained in them, a vague dream of the great work, which gradually over the years grew in them and unconsciously they began to reflect deep within on their lost community. A handful of audacious men made the first move: they visited foreign kingdoms, carried messages; little by little people established friendships, one learnt something from the other; they exchanged their knowledge, their values, their precious metals and they gradually realized that their national languages only distanced themselves from each other and their frontiers were not in fact a chasm between peoples. Their sages came to realize that a science practised by one people could never hope to reach towards the infinite and the scholars soon saw that if they exchanged their knowledge humanity would progress at a faster rate; the poets translated the words of their brothers into their own languages and music, the only art not subjected to the narrow confines of language, served as the common language of emotions. Men loved life more when they knew that, in spite of the obstacle of languages, unity was possible. They thanked God for the punishment he had dealt them and thanked him too for having divided them in such a radical manner, because it gave them the opportunity to relish their world in different ways and to love more consciously their unity with all its many differences.

So the Tower of Babel once more began to rise gradually from the soil of Europe, the monument to communal brotherhood, mankind's solidarity. But it was no longer raw materials which went into this tower's construction, no longer bricks and clay, mortar and earth that they used to reach the heavens and fraternize with God and the world. The new tower was built with a more delicate and yet more indestructible substance which they discovered on earth, that of spirituality and experience, the most sublime material of the soul. Wide and deep were its foundations; Eastern wisdom lent depth, Christian doctrine gave balance, and the humanity of antiquity its building blocks of bronze. Everything humanity had achieved, all that the terrestrial spirit had accomplished was put into this tower, and so it rose up. Each nation contributed to this monument of Europe; the young people rushed in to learn all they could alongside the old, offering their untainted strength to experience and wisdom. They built the tower by hand and the fact that each worked in a different way only fed their communal fervour, for if one achieved more, it encouraged his neighbour to do likewise, and the discord which often threatens nations en masse was powerless to halt the realization of the communal work.

Thus it grew, the new Tower of Babel, and never had its summit reached so high as in our epoch. Never had nations had such ease of access to the spirits of their neighbours, never had their knowledge been so intimately linked, never had commercial relations been so close in forming a formidable network and never had Europeans loved both their homeland and the rest of the world. In this rapture of community, they could already almost touch the sky, for the poets of all languages began in the last few years to celebrate through hymns the beauty of being and creating; and they felt like the builders of that other tower and even like God because they were about to accomplish their work. The monument was growing, the whole of humanity counted on assembling there for the consecration and music resounded around the edifice like a gathering storm.

But God on high, who is immortal like humanity itself, saw with horror that the tower he had destroyed was rising once more, and furthermore he knew that in order to remain more powerful than this humanity he would have to sow discord anew and ensure that men ceased to understand each other. Once more he was cruel, causing confusion to break out amongst them; and so, after thousands of years, this horrific moment appears again in our lives. Overnight men ceased to understand each other, the very same who were peacefully creating together. Because they didn't understand each other they became enraged with one another. Once again they threw down their tools only to use them as weapons instead; the scholars hoarded their own knowledge, the technicians their discoveries, the poets their words, the priests their faith; all that previously had enriched the communal work was transformed into mortal combat.

This is the monstrous moment we are living through today. The new Tower of Babel, the great monument to the spiritual unity of Europe, lies in decay, its workers have lost their way. Still its battlements stand, still its invisible blocks loom over a world in disarray, but without the communal effort to keep the work going it will be entirely forgotten, just like the other in the time of myths. Numberless are the people today who, indifferent to its collapse, believe that their contribution can be withdrawn from the magnificent construction, so that they will reach the sky and eternity through their individual national strength. But some exist who believe that never can a single people, a single nation achieve what a collective of European nations has not through centuries of heroic endeavour, men who ardently believe that this monument must be brought to completion in our Europe, here where it was started, and not in foreign continents like America or Asia. The hour of communal action is not yet upon us, the discord that God has sown amongst us is still too great and years may pass before the conception of a work destined for eternity can be born through peaceful rivalry. But we need to return to the construction site, each to the position he was in when the work was abandoned, when confusion struck. Perhaps we will never see it come to pass, or even hear of it spoken of amongst people; but if we place ourselves there now, each in his allotted spot, expressing the same ardour as in times past, the tower will surely rise again and ultimately all nations will find themselves upon its summit. For this call to work should not come from the pride of individual nations, ever more self-fulfilled in race and language, but rather from the old ancestor, our spirit, which remains the same in all forms, all legends, that nameless builder of Babel, the genius of mankind, whose meaning and salvation it is to strive against his Creator.

HISTORY AS
POETESS

OUR VERY FIRST CONTACT with History dates from
school. It is there children are taught for the first
time that it is not with us that the world begins or began,
but like all organic life it is in a state of constant transformation; the world existed before us and before that
world there was still another. This then is how History
leads us, by our inquisitive child's hand, guiding us ever
further back into the colourful gallery of times past. She
teaches us that there was an epoch where humanity too
was in its infancy, where our ancestors lived without fire,
without light, in caves, like salamanders. But she also
shows before our marvelling gaze how these scattered,
brutal hordes at the beginning gradually gave birth to
peoples, nations, how they crystallized into states, how
from east to west, like a gathering flame, culture spread
from one nation to another and illuminated the world—
step by step, the long road of humanity began its ascent.
Egyptians to Greeks, Greeks to Romans and from the
Romans, across a thousand wars and reconciliations, we
arrive at the threshold of our modern world. History
accomplished her primary task, her eternal task, that
which we all faced in our school years: to illustrate to the
young person, the nascent adult, the origin and development of mankind and thereby link him into an immense

line of ancestors whose work and achievement he must complete in a worthy manner.

As the great governess of world creation—that is how History was presented to us in our youth. But the educators and teachers always wore a severe countenance. For us History was a pitiless judge who, with impassive face, without hate and without love, without judgement and without prejudice, merely engraved with lead pencil, methodically, figures and words, so it seemed to us history was nothing more than an orderly treatment of vast chaos, and we cared little for it. First we had to—and I think this was the same for everyone—learn history by rote, as a duty, before we sought it out for ourselves and began to love it. Most of it was a real bore, very little of this world chronicle appealed, and even then, during our schooldays, our attitude was not altogether devoid of prejudgements and personal predilections. We should remind ourselves that we were not always reading the chronicle, the unfurling story, with the same love and the same interest as now. There were long passages and periods in these history books which we were obliged to learn by heart, without the slightest interest, without joy, without love, without passion, learn them as an obligation, a "school subject", without the participation of our imagination. But then came other episodes which we adored, like so many adventures, chapters where we could not turn the pages fast enough, where our most inward being, our most secret energies were inflamed, where our own fantasy glided into those admired figures, and so we imagined ourselves Conradin, Alexander, Caesar or Alcibiades. I must point out that in this respect at least a

communal experience exists, that for the young of every
country there is a spontaneous choice of preferred period
and figure, and that in every nation and all generations
passion and enthusiasm tend to be directed to the same
episodes and characters. Everywhere it is the great conquer-
ors like Caesar and Scipio who excite youthful admiration
and on the other hand the vanquished heroes like Hannibal
and Charles XII who excite the ardent compassion with
which our youth is so admirably endowed. From north to
south, from east to west, the same dramatic passages tend
to have the same effect on boys of twelve, thirteen, fifteen,
and certain crucial epochs for humanity, the Renaissance,
the Reformation, the French Revolution, seem to implant
themselves in the intellect with a distinct corporeality and
vital imagery. However, it is not by chance that certain figures and certain passages have, since the days of Plutarch,
caused such unanimous inflaming of the imagination. This
secret law, this reason—I see there that this History we
view first as a mistress, an inflexible chronicler, can also
sometimes be a poetess. I must emphasize the word *sometimes*. I say this because it is not so all the time, twenty-four
uninterrupted hours a day, just as is the case with an artist
or poet. Weeks and months can pass, the required fallow
period for all community-building peoples, ordinary citizens
and workers, even the most unproductive lives; all need time
for preparation, the gathering-in. The gradual warm-up
to the poetic craft is just like any other; they must rest and
gather strength, marshal their forces before bursting forth
in triumph. For an individual as much as for a nation the
visionary state can never be habitual and permanent; and

it would be absurd to demand of history, that "mysterious workshop of God", as Goethe called it, that it continuously turn out great, stirring, shocking, gripping events and fascinating personalities. No, history's story cannot simply tell of an endless procession of geniuses, of larger-than-life superhuman characters. It has its remission from tension, its remission from art, and who anyway would wish to read it as one reads a pulp detective novel, where every chapter is laden with gun-toting tension? Surely this would be an offence to the elevated spirit which necessarily permeates it. Let us be firm on this: History cannot be a poetess all the time; she can only, most of the time, play the role of simple chronicler, the clear speaker of facts. It is only on rare occasions that she has her sublime moments, namely those places and personalities which arouse the imagination of youth—in most cases it's mere facts, unfinished material, sober sequential logic, established events. Then sometimes, at the heart of nature, without the interference of man, she forges a pure crystal—and presents in episodes or individuals, or epochs, such a level of tension, such a dramatic perfection that they appear like unsurpassed works of art; and History as poetess of world spirit puts to shame all earthbound poets and mortal spirits.

I would like to try to give another example of these heroic and poetic moments, which I named in one of my books, entitled *Shooting Stars*. Let us consider the European centuries which followed the barbarian invasions. In poetic terms they are not very productive. There are a handful of great figures, such as Attila and Charlemagne, and in Italy the sudden appearance of Dante. But these isolated great figures and their fascinating times, as interesting as they might be, do not meld into that exciting sequence which the true work of art requires. In a work of drama or a novel, it is never enough when the poet introduces only one major figure: a complete work of art must, if it is to excite interest, employ an opposing figure, for each needs the power to develop fully and reveal his true dimensions, which comes from a creative tension. In the same way, History, to articulate its stirring poetical character, must show several great figures at the same moment, and these truly impassioned moments are always uniquely those where some rupture occurs, or where mighty forces collide with destiny, like water plunging over a rock. For years it flows normally with an almost monotonous rhythm, then in a few sublime moments its banks suddenly draw together, a cataract arises, a raging torrent, feverish excitement, and at a stroke the historical scene consummates itself and over-flows with a whole crowd of inspired contrasting figures.

Let us take by way of example the overcrowding of the historical scene during the epoch of Charles V. For centuries Europe had been fragmented. Suddenly, in a single blow, the greatest power disposed to any man fell into the hands of *one* monarch, *one* man. Charles V was at the same time King of Spain, Emperor of Germany, Lord of Italy, of Flanders, of Austria, possessor of a whole world of colonies; he could proudly state that his was an empire on which the sun never set. Had such an extraordinary profusion of dramatic moments ever been forged in so short a time by any power? It formed a vast tableau, poetry of colossal dimensions, bringing to the

fore a number of fascinating and dynamic leading players, providing the prince with adversaries worthy of his
own qualities, genuine monarchs. So in a short space of
time Charles V faced three great rivals: François I, King
of France, Suleyman, the all-powerful Padishah of the
Turks, and Henry VIII of England. But three princes,
even as allies, were not enough to destroy such a mighty
power over a period of twenty years. So then History,
be bolder! Be unstinting! To bring down Charles V *new*
explosive forces needed to emerge, on the heels of the
hitherto unrivalled explosive power of gunpowder and the
printing press. These forces gathered in the shape of the
soul of a minor Augustinian monk named Martin Luther.
This man stood up out of the people and, the pen his only
weapon, totally laid waste to the unity of the Catholics.
The drama really took off when opposing forces entered
the fray; an army of rebels with Thomas Müntzer at its
head caused an insurrection and the Reformation saw
Charles V, the most powerful man on earth, mercilessly
defeated. On an icy winter's night, abandoned by all his
loyal lieutenants, he was forced to flee across the mountains and find sanctuary in a Spanish monastery. What
artist, what poet could have dreamt up a more thrilling
spectacle, where the most powerful man on earth becomes
the only one in an endless line of princes who had reigned
for centuries willingly and with humble abhorrence to
relinquish power? Could any outcome be as logical but at
the same time as surprising as this one? And what a cast
of supporting players makes up this drama! I'll mention
a few names and facts: Luther, Zwingli and Calvin, the

great reformers; Titian, Michelangelo, Benvenuto Cellini, Leonardo and their Rome, defiled, destroyed, its artworks stolen; Machiavelli and Erasmus in Rotterdam; Holbein and the great German masters; Cervantes, whose arm was broken in a storm during the naval battle off Algeria; the discovery of new land in America, the spread of printing across the entire globe; the grotesque scenes during the absurd episode of Anabaptism, the tragedy of the peasants' revolt and the Fiesco conspiracy: dozens, hundreds of such dramas assembled into a living space of thirty years—thirty years so dense with magnificent upsurges and calamitous downfalls, only to be compared perhaps with our own epoch since 1914. This is how History creates poetry, in her "Michelangeloesque" moments.

Or let's view another fresco: the French Revolution, which in five years disintegrated and transformed as much historical matter as a whole century—an epoch that manages to express each phase of thought and feeling in a living person. I am thinking now of the following figures: Mirabeau, the true statesman, Danton, the agitator, Robespierre, the cold and clear-sighted politician, Marat, the demagogue, and alongside them, in all their infinite variety and nuances, a whole host of idealists and the corrupt, a wild maelstrom of wills, permanently locked in struggle with one another. And that unimaginable walk to the guillotine, with each of the condemned following the one before, each knowing that there is yet another awaiting the same fate behind him. What a dance of death worthy of Holbein; and it rampages on and on and on, until due to its own overstretch it finally expires and the heir Napoleon attempts to reach out his hand and snatch the abandoned throne.

And Napoleon in his turn, what a prodigious and un-rivalled invention of History! As a young student at military school he happens to write on a sheet of paper: "St Helena, a tiny island that lies in the Atlantic", unaware that twenty years later his path will lead him to that very place, from all the great battlefields of Europe and the most formidable power one man has possessed since Charles V, and that he will lose it all just as suddenly as his illustrious predecessor.

Here, then, it seems a moment of history is to be repeated. And yet no; nothing ever happens in the same way twice. History is so rich in material that she can always draw new situations and hypotheses from her inexhaust-ible arsenal. She never repeats, she only transposes, like a musician transposing a theme. Of course, sometimes we think we see analogous situations, but this is merely an illusion; and woe to the head of state who allows himself to be steered by these superficial analogies and thinks to act according to a rigid schema, who imagines he can manipulate a current situation by mimicking an event in the past. Louis XVI tried this when the Revolution broke out; he thought he could act wisely by studying books showing how his predecessor Charles I conducted himself during Cromwell's Revolution. This is how he hoped to save his head. But precisely because he wanted to avoid the same mistakes and was too conciliatory, he committed others. History will never allow you to guess the path she will take, for she is too richly endowed for repetitions. She even surpasses the poet or writer who composes a poem, a novel or tragedy, who does not allow the reader or listener to guess the denouement until the last possible moment, who makes reality out of what seems most unlikely, and again and again History exceeds the greatest of expectations. The course of history is always unpredictable and is as random as roulette or any other game of chance, for the events that happen do so in the midst of dimensions and circumstances so unimaginable that our poor human reason cannot possibly foresee them. "There is no past," Goethe says. "One would like to look back, but there is only the eternal new, formed from the spreading elements of the past." History sometimes plays with resemblances, but she never remains the same, she always finds the new, the cloth she cuts is a world cloth; unfailingly she invents, and complete imaginative freedom is permitted her by God; she alone is sovereign among the artists, plays with absolute liberty in this world where all else submits to laws and boundaries. She alone is free and makes use of this freedom in the most profound and sagacious ways. We owe her a little more respect, this elusive poetess! Eternally she will remain our mistress, a paragon we can never reach!

For there is no art or technique which is foreign to this great poetess of History: in every artistic form she presents the definitive example. I showed how, in the time of Charles V or the French Revolution, she created vast frescoes containing hundreds of figures and events, each a drama in itself; how, like Michelangelo, in a great painting she places heaven and hell in the most fantastic contrasts. And even when she is concerned with a less turbulent epoch, where the drama is less condensed, she still shows herself a consummate artist. She does not always have to be stirring to be great. An example of this more *gradual* development: the early history of Rome, in the descriptions of Livy and Sallust. I know of nothing else in all Roman literature which can compare with its clarity of composition, measured growth and unrelieved tension, this calm yet continuous process which in three or four centuries had made of a little village in Latium, a mere molehill, the powerful city we know, centre of the Occident and the cultivated world. In this development of Rome, History eschews romantic, emotive, dramatically taut artistic forms and by contrast demonstrates in a clear account an epic exposé in the grand style, like those Tolstoy has created within the last century.

It's not only when she is emotive that History proves herself a great artist. In those moments admittedly her technique seems more visible, but she also reveals herself to the connoisseur in more modest forms. Let us not forget that History is not overly self-admiring, and that sometimes it happens that she pens a crime or detective novel, like the history of the false Demetrius, the Gunpowder Plot or the affair of Marie Antoinette's necklace; and sometimes she cannot resist farce, the burlesque, as in the case of a swindler duping his time, like Cagliostro or John Law—the world will be none the wiser—or today's gold-makers, Captain von Köpenick, or the thief of the *Mona Lisa*. All art forms, the most elevated to the most playfully popular—History masters them all with the same ease. Likewise she can—whether in the time of the troubadours or of Werther—express with wonderfully touching delicacy the religious turmoil of the time of the Flagellants, the Crusades, the iconoclasm of Savonarola. She knows how to show heroism in all its excesses, where the heroes are desperadoes, as in the conquest of Mexico or that of Siberia by a handful of men who could fit into a single railway carriage. Then History can take on a darker tone, composing sombre war ballads, like poems, so rounded, so enclosed, about the return of Charles XII from Sweden to the Ukraine, or the expeditions of the Vikings, or the fall of the Goths in Italy. But as much as History creates the highest lyrical and dramatic forms, she can, when the mood takes her, resort to simple jokes, to anecdote, and even in this form the situations she presents are incomparable. Everywhere, in all artistic manifestations, in the fresco of characters, she leaves far behind in her wake the fully achieved works of the individual artist or poet.

But how, even though History has made perfect poetry of herself, is there always this seemingly endless procession of writers and artists who seize on historical matter and transform it through their own imagination, thereby creating from raw history dramas and historical novels, and desire to be greater poetical interpreters than reality itself? How do these audacious creators dare to surpass History through invention, she who is the unrivalled mistress of invention, and the supreme poetess? Nothing is more justified than this question, than this objection. Well, we should remember what was noted earlier—that History is not *always* a poetess; there are fallow periods, developments which are too sprawling and ponderous in their evolution, untilled areas amidst this vast field, and—this is decisive—it must be remembered that what History transmits to us is never the whole event, the complete image of man, but merely a shadow of his nature, always fragmentary. Even the individual, each and every one of us, knows particular important things and events and carries them with him to the grave. What it is to have such an abundance of things and events at such a distance from us in time! History, I repeat, is never a finished printed book which we can read from one end to the other, but a vast palimpsest, a compilation, a manuscript of which nine-tenths is amended, where hundreds of pages are indecipherable, and thousands of others are missing and can only ever be replaced in their context through synthesis and the imagination. These countless enigmatic passages must inevitably encourage the poet's addendum, his fabrication. He will attempt to intervene and, following the sense of History, will try as far as he is able to add what is missing, thereby achieving what Michelangelo did with a Greek statue when he tried to replace the arms and head with his own sculptural vision of being. Of course, it is only in the more obscure passages that the poet will seek to apply his imagination to proceedings, not to those that are perfectly clear. In these brilliant passages he does not seek to outdo History. Even the greatest of all poetic dramatists, Shakespeare, inclines to this rule. At the climax of the tragedy of *Julius Caesar*, in Mark Antony's speech when he calls to the people for vengeance, almost word for word the historical text comes straight from Plutarch. If a master such as Shakespeare requires of himself to show such veneration, should it not be required of all? Happily, this respect for the facts, for the original historical material is reborn and the era of the "historical novel", the blatant falsification of our ancestors' lives, is now over. The time is over where a Walter Scott could rearrange history to suit his own needs and form characters who resemble gaily painted marionettes; today it would be unthinkable to do as Schiller, who depicted the young Maid of Orléans falling on the field of battle instead of perishing at the stake. Things have become purer, clearer, more objective and precise, ultimately more honest through our modern way of thinking; we no longer feel obliged to "romanticize" and satisfy the "heroic", to recognize the beauty in a particular historical figure, and we venerate the truth in history too much to modify it casually for our own ends. Who after all has the right to invent a life of genius? One must be a genuinely great poet even to dare, in a work of theatre or a novel, to place *fictional* words in the mouth of a Caesar or a Napoleon, a Luther or a Goethe. Such sacrilege is perhaps admissible when Shakespeare has Julius Caesar speak, or Strindberg Luther. In this case the sensibility of the author is so profound that he really can speak with a kind of fraternal genius. But essentially there are very few who have this right and that is why the vast majority of all that is offered us by way of historical novel or story is nothing more than caricature, a valueless hybrid form, and in the end a literary failure. For if our intellectual power is limited, then the logic of History rests with the spirit of the world. Our dimensions originate from a rigid corporeality, while those of History draw on the armoury of the eternal; and therefore these novelistic inventions mostly treat their heroes on their own level: they dilute elements of the story to make it more digestible to their audience while disregarding History and their own contemporaries.

It is this ignorance of the poetic superiority of History that we witness so clearly in the current trend for the "*biographie romancée*", that is to say, the biography decked with the romantic garnishing of a novel, where the real is intermingled with the false, the documentary with the imaginary, where great figures and events are illuminated by a private form of psychology instead of by the pitiless logic of History. In these romantically infused biographies artifice retouches the canvas, exaggerating the "tiny" traits, reinforcing the heroic and more interesting. But by doing this they produce more posters than psychological portraits in the manner of the great masters. I always prefer the historically accurate biography which does not spin tales but *renounces* all manner of invention, one which humbly *serves* the superior spirit of History and does not stand brash and headstrong in her way. The true biography is that which is content to explain what is happening, respectfully to follow the half worn-away runic traces and, instead of presumption, prefers to state sincerely: "*Nescio*, here I do not know the truth, I cannot be decisive." But through this renunciation the strictly objective historical biography does not become a sterile collection of documents, a cold and passionless after-account. For, naturally, anyone who wishes to get a handle on history must in some sense be psychological: they must possess the faculty of deep perception, of listening closely to the event with the inner ear to have the capability of knowing how to distinguish historical *truths*. This is not a slip of the tongue when I speak of historical *truths*. In history there is virtually never a single and unique truth, but each vital fact is gathered, related to others and transmitted in a hundred different ways. I should recall that famous episode of Walter Raleigh, the great English naval hero and pirate, who, incarcerated in the Tower of London, began to write his memoirs. He begins poring over contemporary accounts of naval warfare, and finds that the battles in which he was engaged are described in a completely different way to what actually happened. He is so disturbed by this that he gravely doubts whether any true historical account is possible and in disgust casts his manuscript onto the fire. This anecdote, so cherished by Goethe, is most instructive, for it demonstrates what we know from psychology: that truth, like the artichoke, has many layers and more often than not behind each truth another lies hidden. There is no definitive chronicle that will account for the soul's actualities, no absolute truth protocol for the historical—and here I return to my theme—for it must always, at least to some extent, be something imagined. The purely material assemblage of facts brings only contradictions; a certain synthetic lens has always been necessary and always will be. The sculptural work always comes from the human; never can the cold specialist gain access to this life force, this quickening of truth, if he does not possess an atom of the poet in him, the seer, the visionary. This is why we can say that in all the areas where history appears uninteresting, it is more the fault of the historian than history itself, for it has not been communicated in a sufficiently poetic way. If we observe history with eyes wide open, as the poet does, we will find that there are no uninteresting figures. No one, even the smallest, most anonymous, most modest character, once the truthful poet's gaze has rested upon him, is dull or indifferent to other men and there are no dull or dead periods of the past either, only poor historians. And, to explain more forcefully, I would say: there is perhaps no actual history in itself, in a general sense, but it is only through the art of writing, the vision of the narrator, when the very factual date of history is *willed*; for every experience and incident only becomes genuine in terms of the senses, when it is recounted in a truthful and verisimilar way. There are in fact no great or small events, only ones that remain alive or are dead, which are remodelled or are past.

Here is an example. Around 3,000 years ago, numberless peoples were dispersed around the Mediterranean and yet we are only properly informed of two: the Greek and the Jewish cultures. The rest have vanished. Why do we only know about these two peoples? Were they somehow greater and more important than all the others? Did more events happen to them than their neighbours? Not at all. Solon the wise was mayor of a small town, barely more significant than a village of today, and the battles between Sparta and Rome, between the Jews and the Amalekites were little more than tussles between parishes. Yet all this has preserved a grandiose and vivid portrait in our memory; it belongs to our deepest sense of history, and the Battle of Marathon, that of Salamis, the conquest of Thermopylae and the taking of Jericho form part of our intellectual knowledge. Each of us has an image of these events engraved on his soul. Why? Not because they were important facts in geographic or numerical terms, but because the Bible on the one hand and the Greeks on the other knew how to recount them in an incomparably splendid and imaginative way, for the poetic expectation had been wholly fulfilled. We see here, and a thousand times more: great actions, great exploits are never enough on their own; a double action is always necessary—the great fact *and* the great narrator, the exciting figure *and* the imaginative performer. Achilles was nothing more than a simple, bold, strong swashbuckler, a hundred of whom can be found in every town and thousands more in every people, from the Papuans to the Iroquois; but only this Achilles became the global hero because Homer saw him as great and presented him thus: the poet transformed him into a legendary mythical character. Consequently, the only way to preserve such events is to re-form them into poetic history. It alone, like the secret of embalming practised by the Egyptians, preserves the colourful over millennia. All the caliphs and princes of antiquity and the Middle Ages knew that any action could not remain alive without a skilful storyteller; that's why they had all their bards, their troubadours and chroniclers. Caesar, Napoleon and Bismarck lost no time in writing the facts of their lives themselves in order that their future legend would accord with their own taste; and our statesmen and diplomats of today know this equally well, which is why they maintain such a healthy rapport with journalists and willingly grant them interviews. These last know that all that happens in the world has no chance of existing for posterity unless the account is forged with the legendary in mind, even at the expense of truth. For men and entire peoples have a craving for legends; I would even dare to say that one key element for a great man is that he creates around himself a poetic aura, an atmosphere of legend, where again and again posterity attempts to reconstitute poetically his character or explain it psychologically. Certain figures such as Napoleon, Gustav Adolf and Caesar will always attract new dramatic and epic poets. Their psychological impetus appears undiminished even after many centuries; it just continues, like a tree which always gives out new leaves at the appropriate time.

But what is true of individuals is also true of nations, for are they not simply collective individuals? A nation gains more power in the spiritual space, the more poetically it can present its historical existence and development in the world. It is not enough that a people might have achieved great things in the domain of culture or war—that is only half of it. The Skipetares of the Balkans, warring for centuries and in a permanent state of insurrection, thereby take a leading role in the history of our world culture, for they knew how best to present the poetic element in their own deeds, raising the life of their people to the level of a saga, a graphic myth. What counts in the contemporary world, as in the past, is not the numeric superiority of a people, nor the tally of its war dead, nor the vastness of its destroyed areas, but that each people profits from universal history, by the value it contributes in terms of artistic sculpturing to the poetic arsenal of humanity. It is not warring peoples who decide, but the *poetic* peoples, and what is decisive in this sense is not the importance of the mass of humanity, but humanity in terms of its creative claim.

I shall take the example of the Scandinavian countries, whose destiny, over centuries, since Charles XII, ceased to have any bearing on the warmongering, imperialist shaping of Europe. Yet with what sculptural force, with what powerful reality are they ever present! As we know their history, their cultural developments, so we sense their presence, through the knowledge that Scandinavian literature conquered Europe at the close of the nineteenth century, that Sweden and Norway possessed for a time an uncontested supremacy in the art of the essay and that their men of letters exercised a primary influence in all Europe. Thanks to Strindberg, to Selma Lagerlöf, to Verner von Heidenstam and a number of others, we have been informed of the historical, sociological and ethnic problems of Sweden as if we were living them ourselves, because poets have spoken of them, because the history and culture of this country have been articulated to us not in a dry and flat academic manner, but in poetic form. Even those countries numerically inferior, poorer or more insignificant in a political, economic or military sense, can make their presence equally felt in world history; and we Austrians feel with the same pride that it is not necessary to be politically challenging or especially rich and powerful economically in order to make our mark on the world with our own cultural life. It is enough that via music the breath of a whole people can be animated, that its being can be opened up to the world, because music harbours this mysterious poetic accent which has the power to render everything that exists with greater substance and reality. I say again that history only lives where it achieves a certain poetic grandeur, which is why the highest accomplishment of a people is to transform as much as possible of its *national* history into *world history*, its private people's myth into a world myth. What ultimately counts are the spiritual values a single nation can offer humanity as a whole. My hope is that the hour is not far off when the nations will only compete in the sense of giving something back to each other, when one can convince the other of its *raison d'être* not through military might but through artistic talent, and history will no longer be recounted via the immortal war ballad but will raise all to a common height with a heroic hymnal poem to unity.

I have sought to present history as "the workshop of God", as an art studio without rival, an archive of the most uplifting and stimulating documents. But what we might say in favour of the past must not make us blind as regards the present. Admittedly, the present is not so easy to warm to: rarely has it been the fate of a generation to live in such a tense and overheated atmosphere as ours, and we all experience a craving to rest a while from the constant overabundance of events which our epoch produces, to take a breath amidst the unremitting political assault to which we are subjected. But precisely if we know world history, if we grow to love it, we can take courage from the present in remembering that *in the long run* nothing that happens is entirely senseless, that all which in past epochs seemed to be useless and senseless to the contemporary mind was later seen from a higher perspective as revealing a creative idea or extolling some metaphysical sense. This is why all the confusion and distress we experience today are but waves bearing us to something new, to the future—nothing is in vain. Each moment that we live, as soon as we give word to it, becomes past. There is no present that does not immediately become history, and thus we are all, as actors and fellow players, endlessly blended into a great drama which is in a perpetual state of becoming; let us then in suspense and awe await its solution. Whoever loves history as a poetic work brimming with soul must equally consider the present and his own existence as also possessing a profound sense and believe, despite current evidence to the contrary, that in the conscious act of creating, acting, writing, we fulfil the real life goal, each of us someone else but all of us the same, that supreme objective, the great triumph over time for which Goethe provides such an admirable formula: "It is to make us eternal that we are here."

EUROPEAN
THOUGHT IN
ITS HISTORICAL
DEVELOPMENT

H ISTORY, this seemingly tideless ocean of events, in fact obeys an unswerving rhythmic law, an internal swell which divides the epochs through ebb and flow, in forward and backward currents—and how could it be otherwise, given that it is created by man and his psychic laws only reflect those of the individual? In each of us this duality exists; the process we call life is in the end only a state of tension between opposing poles. Fortunately we are able to name these opposing forces as the centrifugal and the centripetal, or, in the language of the new psychology, the introvert and the extrovert, or, in that of morals, the egoistic and the altruistic—and it is always through this formula that we express the shifting tendency which is in each of us, on the one hand with the "I" isolated from the world and on the other the "I" bound to the world. We want to retain our "I", the unique personality, who we are, to make this personality still more personal. But simultaneously this personality, this substance which binds us to the world, our individuality, is drawn inexorably into the community. What then is a people other than a collective of individuals? So, underlying all nations is this double tendency: on the one hand their individuality, their spirit and cultural personality, coloured by nationalism, and on the other the supranational search for a higher community which will enrich them but which will demand in return a measure of their wealth and personality. Across all history, these two tendencies of attraction and repulsion, peace and war, the concentric and the expansive, proceed in eternal opposition. As soon as the great structures of state and religion are built they dissolve; over decades and centuries periods of hostility are succeeded by those of reconciliation and friendship; but essentially humanity, with its ever-expanding vision, has always striven towards unions which are more elevated and illuminative. Both of these tendencies, the national and the supranational, already have, since they exist, their cultural and corporeal sense; one is not possible without the other in the intellectual organism of beings that we call states or nations. This opposition is necessary in order to maintain a creative tension at the heart of humanity. But I shall take only one as the object for my study here, in an epoch of nationalist disunity. I wish to underline the contrasting element of unity, that mysterious Eros which has always drawn humanity over differences in language, culture and ideas towards a superior union. I wish to attempt, by casting a glance at the intellectual development of Europe, to furnish a brief history of this perennial yearning for unity, in feelings, wills, thoughts and lives, which across two millennia has created the magnificent common edifice which we can proudly name European culture.

I say "across two millennia". But in truth this basic instinct for an eventual creative community reaches well beyond the history we know, to the primitive times of myths. Already in the most ancient book of the world, at the beginning of the Bible, when it speaks of the first men, we find through a magnificent symbol the first signs of this desire for the creative union of humanity. It is of course the profound legend of the Tower of Babel, and it is this myth that I wish to recall here and explain a little. At that time, having barely departed a state of ignorance, men—whom we might call humanity—had gathered to undertake a communal work. Above them they saw a sky, and because they were men they already experienced the sense of the superhuman, the beyond, so they said to themselves: "Let us build a city and a tower, whose summit will touch the sky, in order that we might secure our place in eternity." And they set to work as one, kneading clay and firing bricks, and began to build their first colossal work.

But God gazed down from heaven—so says the Bible— at this ambitious striving and realized the magnificent scale of the work. He recognized the greatness of the spirit with which he had endowed his creature man, and the extraordinary strength which existed, irresistibly, in this humanity, as long as it remained as one. And in order that humanity was not presumptuous, the Creator decided to obstruct the work and said: "Let us confuse them, so that none knows the language of the other." And the Bible states that the men's work quickly foundered, since they could no longer understand each other; and because of this they became angry and irritable among themselves. They threw down their bricks, their trowels and other tools and fought each other; then they abandoned their half-begun work, each returning to his home and town. They cultivated their own ground and stayed in their own homesteads, professing love for their country and language alone. Thus the Tower of Babel, a communal work of all humanity, remained deserted and fell into ruins.

This myth taken from the opening pages of the Bible is a wonderful symbol of the idea that with humanity as a community all is possible, even the highest aspirations, but only when it is united, and never when it is partitioned into languages and nations which do not understand each other and do not want to understand each other. And perhaps— who knows what mysterious memories can still be traced in our blood?—there is still some vague reminiscence in our spirit of those distant times, the Platonic memory of when humanity was united and the persuasive, haunted longing that it might eventually recommence the unfinished work; in any case, this dream of a unified world, a unified humanity, is more ancient than all literature, art and scientific knowledge.

A legend, a childish myth, a heroic fable—but what was it our great master of psychology Sigmund Freud taught us on the subject of myths? That they are nothing more than the wish dreams of a people, no different to an individual's dreams, which are merely expressions of the unconscious and conceal a desire hidden deep within. Never are dreams, especially those of whole generations, completely futile. We should trust in these myths of primitive epochs. For each idea which occurs was formerly a dream, and all we invent and realize now was simply what our courageous forefathers desired or longed for before us.

But let us depart from the vestibule of legend and enter the inner sanctum of history. In its earliest beginnings there was unrelieved darkness. Then we see, on the shore of the Mediterranean and in the east, empires begin to form, then disappear, their destiny sometimes down to the will of a single man, an Alexander, or that of a whole people concentrated in a force so powerful it spreads like a tide across different countries, but only to plunder, ravage and destroy them; and when this warrior tide draws back there is left only the silt of decay. Those civilizations born at the dawn of history possessed no edifying or organizational powers; they did not yet serve the idea of community, and even the Greek civilization did not stamp the seal of unity on the world. There was a measure of it, and it was new and wondrous for the human soul, but it was not bestowed on humanity. The true political and intellectual unification of Europe only began with Rome and the Roman Empire. Here for the first time a city was established, a language and, through law, the will to govern and administer all peoples, all nations of the world under a single system, brilliantly worked out—domination not only by force of arms but on the basis of a spiritual principle, domination not as an objective in itself but for the intelligent organization of the world. With Rome, Europe had for the first time a unified format—and one might say for the last time, for never was the world so unified as in that distant epoch. A single plan, a visionary plan, stretched like an ingenious network across the countries of Europe, still uninformed and devoid of culture, from the cloudy isles of the Britons to the blistering sands of the Parthian Empire, from the columns of Hercules to the Black Sea and the steppes of Scythia. One single system of administration, of finances, military organization, justice, morals, science, and a single language, Latin, dominated all others. On the roads constructed with Roman technology, marching behind the legions came Roman culture, a methodical and constructive spirit to succeed one of unthinking destructive force. Where the sword had cleared the land, language, laws and morals were sown and germinated. For the first time Europe's chaos was replaced by unified order, a new idea was born, the idea of civilization, of humanity managed according to moral principle. If this edifice had held out for two or three centuries more, the roots of peoples would have been inexorably intertwined and the unified Europe which is today a mere dream would have been a reality, and all continents discovered later would have fallen in line with the central idea.

But precisely because this Roman Empire was so huge, so sprawling and so deeply anchored to the European soil, its unravelling signified nothing less than a moral and spiritual catastrophe, a collapse without parallel in the history of European culture. From this standpoint, the fall of the Roman Empire can only be compared to a man who, following a terrible convulsion of the brain, has suddenly forgotten everything that happened before, and from a mature intellectual state falls into one of complete imbecility. Communication between peoples ground to a halt and roads fell into disrepair; towns became depopulated, for a common language and Roman organization no longer linked the countries. The new colonies, like the old, forgot over an incredibly short period of time all they had known: art, science, architecture, painting, medicine—they all dried up overnight like springs following an earthquake. In a single blow European culture fell far below that of the

Orient and China. Let us recall this moment of European shame; literary works were burnt or sat rotting in libraries. Italy and Spain were forced to hire their doctors and scholars from the Arabs and clumsily and onerously learnt art and trade from the Byzantines. Our great Europe, teacher of civilization, had to go back to school and be taught by her own pupils! A great heritage was needlessly wasted, statues were destroyed, buildings were razed, aqueducts collapsed and the roads were left in a state of dereliction. This tragic epoch was even unable to recount its own history, while only 400 years earlier Tacitus, Livy, Caesar and Pliny described theirs so artfully.

This moment is the culminating point of Europe's fragmentation, the lowest point of our communal culture, the most withering blow that it has ever received. It is truly horrifying to recall this epoch—horrifying, because you are gripped by the fear that, once again and with a similar blow, the new edifice to which we have all contributed a stone might collapse through the same spiritual and moral upheaval and its catastrophic effects be loosed on the world. But let us not forget: even in the very moment of extreme anarchy, Europe did not completely jettison the idea of unity. For this idea is indestructible. Like the human body when it opposes murderous germs within its own blood, the organism called humanity, in moments of grave danger, draws from itself an equable curative strength. In the epoch where the earth has been devastated and then delivered from the elements of destruction, the spirit builds a new construction; for at the very moment the Roman Empire collapsed, the united architectural will of humanity created a new, admirable work, that of the Roman Church, as if it lifted to the clouds a reflection of its earthly power. The material was destroyed but the spirit was saved; the terrible hailstorm had passed; a grain had germinated, the Latin tongue, which rose phoenix-like from the flames. What the hand had built up might collapse, but what the spirit had created from the community of humanity could be obscured, but not lost. Latin, the language of unity, the mother tongue of all European cultures, has been preserved for us even at this apocalyptic hour.

True, the monks salvaged the language from the rabid destruction of the barbarians, hiding it in the catacombs of their cloisters, but the life force of Latin became clouded through this concealment. In the same way that pearls lose their lustre when lacking contact with the warmth of a human body, so Latin, when confined to the scholastic, unused as spoken language, dwindled on the lips of men and lost its international standing. Deprived of air, no longer irradiated by the Italian skies, this Latin language lost its sensuousness, its clarity, its elegance, all the highest virtues which had given us so much joy in the reading of its poets. In this language you could no more rejoice, joke, laugh or speak with finesse and taste of tender and vital things, no more maintain contact with your friends, neither by letter nor by voice. What had once been the language of the world was now only used for scholarly subjects, those "*artes liberales*", and not for general usage. For several centuries all possibility of understanding within Europe was shattered.

A dark slumber weighed on the world of the spirit, a sleep peopled with mysterious dreams and visions. But awaiting its end, already beginning to shine, is a new dawn; already a handful of men are working to imbue Latin, lost in the shadow of theological parchment, with the blood-warmed rays of life, the suppleness of living speech. A whole cavalcade of poets, with Petrarch at its head, infuses the old mummified language with blood and vigour, forming a new alliance around it; a new class of spiritual men of the world, a kind of classical Esperanto.

And all of a sudden the miracle is realized: spiritual men across Europe, separated by the diversity of their national languages, can now correspond with each other again, can write letters and understand each other in a fraternity enabled by language. Frontiers between countries are breached in a wing-beat thanks to the new language. It matters not in the epoch of Humanism whether you study in Prague, Oxford or Paris. The books are in Latin, the teachers speak Latin—*one* art of speaking, thought and social intercourse brings all Europe's intellects under one umbrella. Erasmus of Rotterdam, Giordano Bruno, Spinoza, Bacon, Leibniz, Descartes—they all feel themselves citizens of the same republic, the men of knowledge. Europe feels that once again it is forging towards a new community, a new future of Western civilization. The intellectuals of all nations visit each other, dedicate their books to each other, they discuss—and always together—the problems of the time. With a swiftness which contrasts uncannily with the heaviness and slowness of mail coaches and sailing ships, they share their knowledge, their literary works and the problem that they belong to different nations, the first being a Dutchman, the second a German, the third an Italian, the fourth a Frenchman and the fifth a Portuguese Jew is of less importance than the new-found exhilarating feeling that they are all deputies in an invisible parliament of Europe, that they have a heritage to manage together, that all new discoveries and all ancient spiritual conquests belong to the community. If a forgotten comedy of Terence is found in a hidden corner of Italy, there is a cry of joy in England as in Poland and Spain among the men of intellect, as if a child has been born, or some fortune dropped out of the sky. In this supranational kingdom of Humanism, through this supremacy of an international elite, indifferent to political struggles, guided by artistic passion, feeling themselves above all frontiers, the proof is furnished once more, for the first time since the collapse of the Roman Empire, that communal European thought is possible, and this concept enlivens and animates all minds. It seems to these men that the free world has become wider and richer; from the earth rise up, in the form of statues and speaking the language of former times, the spirits of an ancient world; across the seas old continents emerge, the invention of printing spreads its invisible wings—and likewise, with a richness hitherto undreamt of, the spiritual word. Whenever the world expands, spirits are gladdened, and this exuberance of strength, of pleasure, of life aura finds its greatest and most enduring form in what we now name the Renaissance, in the truest sense of the word a rebirth of the spirit.

This first form of European intellectualism, which we look on with envy, coming as it did after a protracted period of war, brutality and hostility, surely represents one of the high points of humanity. Although separated from one another by thousands of miles, the poets, thinkers and artists of Europe were more intimately connected than today, in the time of aeroplanes, railways and automobiles. The moment of the Tower of Babel, that of the highest human assurance, appeared to have returned.

But, just as pitilessly, after the flow comes the ebb, and these periods of fraternization are replaced by those of conflict and destruction: human nature is unable to exist without direct contrasts. Once again, after the highest summit comes the deepest downward plunge. The cohesion of the Catholic Church, which for more than a thousand years had linked the various countries of Western Europe, fails, the wars of religion begin and the Reformation destroys the Renaissance. With it also dies the sovereignty of that resuscitated body of the Latin tongue, this last symbol of a united Europe. Once again the European idea remains just a torso, an inchoate monument, left behind and forgotten. Through the discovery of antiquity on Italian soil the nations experience a prodigious sense of empowerment, and as always power is transformed into pride. Now each country is keen to achieve political and intellectual hegemony for itself; each wants to create through its own language a literature capable of rivalling that of antiquity. In every people, the poets throw off the communal language, Latin, and create masterpieces in their own: Tasso and Ariosto in Italy, Ronsard, Corneille and Racine in France; Calderón, Cervantes and Lope de Vega in Spain; Milton and Shakespeare in England. A glorious contest then follows, as if each European people felt the duty to prove on the Areopagus of history that they were the one best fitted to lead the direction of world literature after Rome. Nationalistic literature is born, the primary power, still peaceful, of the national consciousness, and for two or three centuries, from the end of the Renaissance to the French Revolution, any fraternal spirit in the arts all but dies out, the flame that Humanism had fanned so ardently and magnificently.

But as I have said from the outset, the impulsion for mutual engagement and confluence is an intrinsic element of the human soul, and nothing issuing from our innermost soul can ever be suppressed. World history knows no pause, no termination; the drive for a higher connection, the communal spiritual life force never falters, it only changes its mode of expression. This finds symbolic form in the civilization of Rome and her language, then in religion, then in Humanism, in the new Latin and in science. Now the common language has fallen into ruin following the awakening of Italian, Spanish, French, English, German, the inclination towards community seeks a new form, and finds it—a new language standing above all others—in music. In the seventeenth and eighteenth centuries it's not the poets, nor the theologians, nor the learned men but the musicians who are the standard-bearers for European unity; these most qualified representatives of cosmopolitanism form a single great fraternal family. Barely have Monteverdi and Palestrina in their "*stile nuovo*" brought a new brilliance and greatness to the language than Europe says to herself: here is a new language through which we all understand each other and so it matters little where the musician lives or where he practises his art, or which language he speaks: *ubi ars, ibi patria.* One nation accords to another the fullest hospitality. Musicians are the great travellers of the seventeenth and eighteenth centuries, the messengers between peoples. Let us not forget how they transform every country: the old Heinrich Schütz goes to Italy to learn from Gabrieli, Handel makes his home in Naples and London, Gluck is sometimes in Vienna and sometimes Paris. One of the sons of the arch-Protestant Bach sets up in Milan, the other in England. The Austrian Mozart is welcomed at the age of fourteen into the Bologna Academy and his most celebrated works, *Don Giovanni, Così fan tutte, Le nozze di Figaro,* raise their immortal Italian words to the very heights of song. But just as the Germans are found in Italy, so the Italians reach all cities of Europe: Porpora in London and Dresden, Piccinni and Cherubini in Paris, Jommelli in Stuttgart, Caldara and Salieri in Vienna, Cimarosa in St Petersburg, and his immortal work *Il matrimonio segreto* was composed in Vienna, in that Vienna where Metastasio wrote operatic texts for musicians of all languages. Handel, Mozart, Haydn, Gluck, Spontini—they write their operas from French, English, German, Italian texts and their correspondence reveals the most colourful variegation of languages. This great cosmopolitan race lives beyond country, language, nation, and feels a sense of pride in its brotherhood. Everything seems united in the common impulse to express human feeling; all are priests worshipping one God, servants to a common enterprise.

As we see, the rhythm of this movement that pushes one people towards another never really stops completely.

A spiritual quality is always discernible whenever the people of Europe are awakened to culture, another form of art—science—always raises the multi-coloured flag of unity; but always violence—sworn enemy of the spirit—ruptures this fraternal sentiment: this time it's the Revolution, then the Napoleonic Wars that give birth to national armies and forge the idea that patriotism is no longer just the business of princes, but of interest to the people. From this, art and thought take on a national character. Once again we see a retreat. With Beethoven and Schubert, and still more with Wagner, Chopin or Mussorgsky, Rossini and Verdi, the supranational in music becomes national and the literature patriotic, a situation which still exists today and which is called intellectual autarchy, the conscious awareness of an isolationist element to the national soul.

But in the very moment of division—over a hundred years of it—a great voice rises, pronouncing with an imperious air these prophetic words: "The times of national literature are over, the time of world literature is upon us." Who says these words? Is it some stateless poet, someone who does not care for his own language, who doesn't understand the feelings of his country, who has no love for it, a "*fuoruscito*", one banished, exiled from his own land? No, it's the greatest of German poets, Goethe. The more this ascending spirit grows and gains clarity, the more space he demands. The German world, the purely German point of view now appears to him, he who spreads his gaze over the whole earth; but alongside his wholly German position he creates a European consciousness and strives, despite being German first, to think of all peoples to the depths of his soul. He says (and his words ring true as if he had said them today): "At the time when man is absorbed in creating new fatherlands, for the man who thinks freely, for him who can raise himself above his epoch, the fatherland is nowhere and everywhere." Goethe's spirit embraces reality but at the same time foresees the future, grandiosely anticipating, at a time when railways and aeroplanes were merely childish fantasies, a future network of nations bound together through technological progress: "the free exchange of ideas and feelings," he says, "is as fruitful for growth as the free exchange of goods for the wealth and well-being of mankind. If that has not happened until now, it is for the lack of firm laws, and the way to these is through robust international relations." What wise words, so profound, reaching beyond the narrow parameters of his own time, words which already by the early years of the nineteenth century proved to be true. Whilst in the fifteenth, sixteenth, seventeenth and eighteenth centuries it took decades for a literary or artistic influence to pass from people to people—Shakespeare was forced to wait 150 years to be translated—in the nineteenth century certain feelings and currents of collective thinking began to appear in Europe; men in France, Germany, Italy and England were showing an equitable spiritual disposition. It is not by chance that the lyrical pessimism of a Byron, a Shelley, a Hölderlin, a Pushkin and a Mickiewicz find similar expression in all countries at the same time, or that in 1848 the same political explosion happened everywhere at the same moment; in former times such flare-ups were separated from one another by decades and centuries. The nineteenth century sees, thinks, feels in an identical way; in all countries one senses a kind of communal psyche evolving above national literatures and national spirit, a world literature, European thought, a spirit of coexisting humanity is coming into being.

Once the spiritual phenomenon is recognized, then we see the intellectual process shine forth and we witness an increase in power to speed up this process. While in earlier times the sense of a European brotherhood, a constellation of cosmopolitan feeling was only occasionally felt at certain moments, by the end of the nineteenth century the prospect of political and extra-political agreements lent credence to the notion of "A United States of Europe". The idea that all countries on this continent could belong to a single economic and spiritual organism has in fact only been in existence for the last half-century. Nietzsche, first among contemporary thinkers, declared resolutely that we must be done with the "fatherlanders" and create a supranational consciousness, the patriotic sentiment of a new Europe. For him, so tragically ahead of his time, there was no discussion possible about the inevitable fact that Europe, "this little peninsula off Asia", as he ironically dubbed it, must ultimately unite. "Thanks to the pathological alienation," he says, "which the nationalistic idiocy has established and still establishes among European peoples, thanks as well to the short-sighted politicians with hasty hands who are on top today with the help of this idiocy and have no sense of how the politics of disintegration which they carry on can necessarily only be politics for an intermission, thanks to all this and to some things today which are quite impossible to utter, now the most unambiguous signs that Europe wants to become a unity are being overlooked or wilfully and mendaciously reinterpreted." You might perhaps say that reality has ferociously stifled this way of seeing between nations for a further quarter-century, due to the outbreak of the most horrifying war humanity has experienced. But this eventuality, which Nietzsche had in some sense foreseen, did not allow him to be shaken in his beliefs: "This process of the formation of the new Europe," he said, "might be slowed by a significant reduction in velocity, but perhaps it will emerge with more depth and intensity." He who has real faith in an idea does not let himself be diverted by isolated facts which seem to contradict his conviction, for a thought, fully recognized in its necessity, has some invincible shock force that, through the intermediary of the war, brought the "depth and intensity" desired by Nietzsche closer in a way the less vigorous formula of Goethe never could. Just as ardently, a few years later, Émile Verhaeren, the great Belgian lyricist, developed in his poetry the idea of the need for a community between European peoples. This poet, existing between two separate linguistic groups, between two great peoples locked in struggle for a century, had been struck profoundly by the fact that on the other side of the ocean Walt Whitman, the "Americano", was being feted as the man of the future. Whitman proclaimed his American people as those who would be dominant in any forthcoming spiritual sovereignty over the earth. This aroused the pride in the great European Verhaeren to issue a response. Should Europe really give way? No, Never! In this still-youthful man, inflamed with ardour, there was something that refused to countenance the idea that Europe, which for 2,000 years had been "*la forge de l'idée*", the sacred forge where all the great thoughts had been hammered out, this incomparable force born of the blood and spirit of all nations—that now this Europe must submit and tender her sword and sceptre to the young pretender. Verhaeren became exasperated with all the chatter over the "decline of the West", as if somehow Europe's mission on earth was now at an end. Verhaeren believed (and we believed with him) in the vitality of Europe and in its strength, which was far from being exhausted; he was of the mind that European nations had a responsibility to safeguard the spiritual direction of the world, but only on condition that we not reduce ourselves, destroy ourselves in futile struggles, but rather bind ourselves through impassioned community. This binding and elevating element between Europe's nation states Verhaeren viewed with generous enthusiasm, expressing candid and joyous admiration for our achievements in such a mutually enabling coming-together.

> *Si nous nous admirons vraiment les uns les autres*
> *Du fond même de notre ardeur et notre foi,*
> *Vous, les pensiers, vous les savants, vous les apôtres,*
> *Pour les temps qui viendront, vous extrairez la loi.*

> If truly we admire one another
> to the depths of our faith, our ardour,
> You, thinkers, you learned men, you apostles,
> You'll find the formula for the coming era.

When we in Europe know no more antagonism, no more pulling rank, if we could just stop underlining our differences in a hostile manner, if we could admire with sincerity the leading influence of one people then another, we might properly pursue that moral force which has always been the decisive one in the history of our time. We must stand united, we men of the West, inheritors of ancient cultures, if we wish to preserve the spiritual direction of the world and accomplish the half-finished task. All our differences and our petty jealousies must be put aside in order that we might achieve this single aim of faithfulness towards our past, and of our community-based future.

So in the period preceding the war, the ideal of a common European way of thinking and doing is nascent: a philosopher proclaims it with rational conviction, then a lyric poet in the fiery fervour of his enthusiasm, and another great work of this epoch also contributes to the idea of a united states of Europe: *Jean-Christophe,* the novel by Romain Rolland. Here a writer attempts to fuse the voices of different peoples into a great symphony and, like Orpheus, to tame the conflict of the elements, thanks to the spirit of music. In this work Rolland allows his hero to say, sadly: "The Europe of today has no communal book, not a poem, a prayer, an act of faith which can be said to belong to us all, and this is shameful, and something which proves devastating for the artists of our time. Not one who writes for all, who thinks for all." It is this deficiency that Jean-Christophe seeks to confront: the antagonism of nations, and the consequent prevention of works that might serve to unify. This novel sells itself as a catechism of mutual understanding, of reciprocal education in the recognition that each nation owes an intellectual debt to another. Jean-Christophe is a German, cloistered in his own country; he has no understanding of other peoples, other nations. He arrives in Paris, finds everything strange, mendacious, fraudulent, preposterous, until he meets a friend, Olivier, a Frenchman, who teaches him to understand the peculiar inner character of French culture. Each learns something from the other, German power from French intelligence, creative action linked to creative thought. But Germany and France are only a duo: that's not enough. So with Gracia a third country enters the scene: after German strength and French lucidity, we have the pure beauty of the Italian genius. "The smile of the Italian sky" suddenly shines over the battleground and brings clarity to the atmosphere with its golden light. It is in Italy, then, that the symphony of this work finds its most musical and humane conclusion. Infused with the spirit of three nations, Jean-Christophe becomes a European; the heights of inner freedom have been reached, a sense of justice, righteousness, which favours reason over pride.

I only cite three works, three men among all those in the period before the war who demonstrated with clear conscience the need for a united Europe. Countless are the others who furtively and silently shared this faith; and from the beginning of the new century, due to closer and closer commercial relations between peoples and the growing wealth of nations, an optimistic voice began to be heard across the continent. Always at moments of great unity, humanity feels empowered by a kind of religious feeling;

in the periods where she rises highest, the distant seems that much closer, and even the inaccessible within easy reach. That's why the young of my generation—we who grew up in the new century and everywhere, in France, England, Italy, Spain and the Scandinavian countries—found new friends and comrades working together for the general reconciliation of peoples, and, guided by our faith, thought that the whole world could be made one through such friendships, that a united states of Europe was already virtually a reality; how such a thought made us rejoice! But it was precisely this generation, those who experienced the uniting of Europe as a kind of evangelism, who were forced to see the total collapse of these hopes with the outbreak of war in Europe. Once again our spiritual Rome was destroyed, once again our Tower of Babel was left abandoned by its artisans.

The deep anguish that this conflict caused among nations we know all too well. Even today bridges remain to be rebuilt, even today these years of destruction create through large swathes of the population a sense of opposition to thoughts of community and brotherhood. But a strange thing is happening—outside of our will and knowledge; for if I were to try to formulate the situation of today I would say that any tendency towards unification is far stronger in *material things* than in the spirit of *mankind* itself. A different kind of spirit to that of poets, seers, philosophers is working now towards universal accord, to world interaction, a wholly impersonal spirit: the spirit of the technological century. This spirit is taking other forms than we have known until now; it is a spirit entirely detached from the individual and belongs wholly to the collective; indeed most of what we call technological progress, which is rapidly transforming the world, perhaps with rare exceptions, answers only to the collective. The technological spirit working today towards the unification of the world is more about a way of thinking than anything to do with humanity. This spirit has no country, no home, no human language; it thinks in formulae, reckons in figures and it creates machines which, in their turn, create us, almost against our will, in an exterior form which is more and more identical. The new art forms lose more and more their national characteristics and take on the collective one. Whether we like it or not, the more our communal technology reduces distances, the more narrowly we proceed in space and time. Does any sense of distance still exist, when it is so effortlessly bridged by aeroplane and an exotic foreign journey can be had through the radio; when, with a twist of the dial, we can tune into London, Rome, Moscow or Madrid? The faculty of being everywhere at one and the same time has been granted us in these recent technological advancements, to a degree our forefathers could never have imagined. What is of importance to a nation can be transmitted in the space of a breath and it is inconceivable that our individual spirit can somehow evade this relentless drive towards the collective. With superhuman force the conquests of technology bring us inexorably closer together; and if there were not this unshakeable impulse towards the individual and that other drive, each nation striving for independence, then we would for a long time now have been a single community. But this opposition, this nationalist tendency has been markedly reinforced by the state of tension in which we now live; resistance has grown proportionately to the pressure, and thus the problem of the struggle between the national and the international, the national state and the super-European state, has climaxed at precisely the most dramatic moment in history.

I felt obliged to show briefly in a rough sketch how, across the centuries, these two currents were always in permanent opposition: that is to say, the affirmation of national independence and the desire for a supranational community. I tried to show how the individual will and that of the community moved in a more or less rhythmical ebb and flow. Today they are locked in a decisive struggle one against the other. Never has the gulf between states been so yawning, more vehement, more conscious, more organized than today: with decrees of all sorts, autarchic economic measures, each nation can resist another in ruthless isolationism. But while they shut themselves off behind their frontiers, these countries remain conscious that their destiny is irrevocably linked to a European economic and political model, that no country can entirely escape, isolating itself from a world crisis, for, as in Goethe's *Faust*, when you bar the doors, trouble enters anyway through the keyhole. Nationalism versus supranationalism—it is the problem from which there is no hiding, and the coming times will tell us if the states of Europe wish to persist in their political and economic hostility, or finally resolve this exhausting conflict through complete union, a superstate. I believe we all feel everywhere today that electric crackle caused by the collision of antagonisms; and nervously we ponder if one of the two tendencies might prevail. But if so, which? Will Europe pursue a path to its own destruction, or will it become united? Forgive me if I do not say that reason will win and tomorrow and beyond we will see a unified Europe, an end to war, to internal politics and this destructive hate between peoples: I do not dare issue such a promise. Please excuse my faintheartedness. Our generation, which for a quarter-century has only witnessed political events directed *against* the rational, which sees key decisions made not at the eleventh hour but at the twelfth, our tested and disappointed race which saw the insanity of war and its aftermath no longer has the childish hope to believe in sane, clear, rapid decisions. It too has recognized the strength of these opposing tendencies, the favouring of short-term interests over the required wider view, the power of egoism pitched against the spirit of brotherhood. No, this united Europe will not happen tomorrow, we may have to wait years, decades, and perhaps our generation will not see it come to pass. But—and I have said this already—a genuine conviction does not need to be confirmed by reality to know it is just and true. And today no one should be denied the right to write his letter from the front as a European, to call himself a citizen of Europe and, in spite of borders, consider the world as a fraternal community. Of course this might all be an illusion. But whoever can somehow raise his thinking above the naked reality of the world as it stands now, will have created a state of personal freedom for himself that flies in the face of our preposterous epoch. He can look on all the posturing and deceiving artistry of long-drawn-out diplomacy with a certain smile playing on his lips; he can mistrust the hate-saturated journalism perpetrated on both sides, abhor the squabbles and rankling between nations and regret with compassion the malodorous intolerance of peoples towards each other. If he can himself look away, hold his breath against the vile hatred which lays across our world today like a cloud of poison gas, and, disassociating himself, wave aside these conflicts, then will he better understand humankind on this earth and elevate himself to a serene, unprejudiced and clearer sense of justice, thanks to which—in the magnificent words of Goethe—he shall perceive the destiny of all peoples as his own.

THE UNIFICATION
OF EUROPE

F OR US WHO HAVE FOUND ourselves here reunited around an idea, I feel there is no longer a need to discuss the necessity and compelling logic of that idea, for to do so would simply be to waste time. All the leading heads of state, intellectuals, artists and scholars have been convinced for some time now that only a slender allegiance by all states to a superior governing body could relieve current economic difficulties, reduce the propensity for war and eliminate anxieties aroused by the threat of conflict, which are themselves one of the primary causes of the economic crisis. Our sole common task, then, is now to shift our ideas from the sphere of sterile discussion to one of creative action.

For that to happen we must first above all understand the exceptional challenges which confront the realization of that idea, for until now it has been the domain, as in the epoch of Humanism, of a selective higher class and its roots have not yet penetrated the earth of the people, so we would be fooling ourselves if we imagined that we were anywhere close to our ultimate objective. Let us first recognize the pre-eminence of nationalism in our epoch. The European idea is not a primary emotion like patriotism or ethnicity; it is not born of a primitive instinct, but rather of perception; it is not the product of spontaneous fervour, but the slow-ripened fruit of a more elevated way of thinking. It entirely lacks the impassioned instinct which fuels patriotic feeling, and thus the sacro-egoism of nationalism will always cut more keenly through to the average man than the sacro-altruism of the European ideal, because it is always easier to be aware, through a spirit of devotion and veneration, of one's own kind than of one's neighbour. Moreover, nationalism has been organizing itself for centuries and has always profited from the support of the most powerful in society. Nationalism can count on the education system, the army, those in uniform, newspapers, songs and insignia, the radio and language; it has the state as its protector and wins the response of the masses, while in the service of our idea we have only the word and writing, which (one can hardly deny) proves woefully ineffectual against many centuries of nationalism's tried and tested formula. With books and pamphlets, with conferences and discussions, we only ever reach a tiny minority of this European community, and even then we are merely preaching to the converted; what's more, we equally fail to employ modern technical and visual channels to further our cause. Let us take today's discussion. Perhaps a brief extract will appear tomorrow in a newspaper, lost between a hundred other items of news, and over this extract millions of cursory and indifferent eyes will skim in an instant; and tomorrow, when we are keen to test public reaction, enquiring of the taxi driver who is taking us home or when we are at the kiosk buying cigarettes, we become aware that, even in the city where the conference took place, the anonymous mass is completely oblivious to our endeavours. We were perhaps too hasty in imagining that what we took for decisive action was in fact little more than a gesture, a fine but futile gesture, the same one that each generation of scholarly elites has performed down the centuries.

If our idea is to have any tangible effect, we must recover it from the esoteric domain and devote all our energy to making it more visible and persuasive to a wider circle. To this end, the word alone is not enough, and we need to harness all the fomenting diffusive forces of our time to make our ideas more visually compelling to the masses. We should recognize and admire how nationalism, already manipulating the state's levers of power, flaunts its artistic and theatrical mastery: recall if you will the speech by Mussolini before 200,000 souls this 1st May on Tempelhof field, or the million assembled on Red Square in Moscow, where some two million workers and soldiers marched in an uninterrupted procession for hours on end; and let us learn from these examples that the masses are most jubilant when they feel themselves visible and can display themselves en masse. In all this mass behaviour a hypnotic force is at work, whilst a frenzy of exaltation rises into which no authentic thought can penetrate. Never through the mere reading of a brochure or newspaper can the true depths of a nation be properly demonstrated. If we cannot arouse such enthusiasm for our idea, there, in the heart and blood of peoples, our formula will be in vain, for never in the history of change has the intellectual sphere and that of patient reflection ever triumphed. We must, then, before all else, give visibility and passion to our idea, transform it from pure ideology to one of practical organization which goes beyond mere logic and shows a more demonstrative character. It is in this eminently practical and organizational form that all our thoughts and propositions must now be concentrated and each of us must acquire a new perspective to meet all practical and psychological contingencies.

Allow me to attempt to put to you a proposal which moves in this direction and which may permit us better to visualize our idea.

The tragedy of our European idea is that it has no stable central foundation on which to stand. Our Europe lacks a capital city, for Geneva, which should play this role, never became a capital like Washington, but remained a conference place, the sterile assemblage of emissaries from all states, a gathering not of the people but of diplomats—who form a necessarily narrow elite. What happens there and what is decided never touches the feelings of the masses nor taps the lifeblood of nations. Geneva has never become popular, and the Slovakian worker, or the Norwegian sailor, to the extent that he has even heard the term "League of Nations", does not associate with it one iota of his feelings; his passions are not aroused, he lacks the optical, the visual, the tactile aspects of these political and economic discussions. And, I repeat, until the European idea achieves these basic forms of the visible and tangible, of what we can feel passionate about, until it becomes for people a sort of patriotism and supranationalism—until then it is doomed to remain sterile and it will never manage to become reality. We must above all else locate a central idea which is visually recognizable!

Allow me to submit to you such a proposal; I would naturally be happy if you judged it appropriate, but I would be even happier if it could be surpassed by something better or more efficient, or at least trimmed down. I have just emphasized that supranational links already exist in diverse forms. Every year sees sporting events bringing all nations together and hundreds of international conferences, of doctors, theologians, workers, writers, bank directors, sociologists, physicians, technicians, post-office employees, poultry farmers, philosophers, wine merchants—I list these professions in a rather preposterous manner, a small section of an interminable list, for there is not a group or a class in our eternally diverse world which does not find itself gathered each year for a conference of one kind or another. Each time, through these meetings, vital contacts are forged, emboldened by a sense of the European. Each time at these events a small circle becomes conscious of the need for a supranational entente. But it is only ever an isolated bloom which blossoms and then fades as quickly without anyone even noticing, lost as it is in the sprawling machinery. With all these conferences, the effect of visibility, that visual element that I deem so necessary, can only last a day, maybe only an hour; our reunion today, it too will fall fatally into the sphere of transience. But if an organization—and this is my suggestion—could arrange for every international congress to be held in such a way that they proceeded, regularly one after another and at all times throughout the year, in one particular city for a month, then surely the chosen city for that month would acquire the visibility of a European capital. The fact that all the workers, the legal profession, the scholars, dentists, clerks, farmers, all the inhabitants of the town could, for this month, each in their area of expertise, feel themselves linked to foreign lands, means that this town could really be infected by our European idea. This feeling would spread to the region and surrounding countries and for months after, even years, they would still remember that great moment lived as one community. The same force that habitually loses its strength through being fragmented and scattered would gather itself in a single great expository act which would be deemed of great significance, since men rarely conserve the memory of a great event in their country unless they clothe it in a solemn character. Let us suppose, then, that one day all the conferences over one year might be booked for Helsinki, Prague or Lyons, Hamburg or Glasgow (I exclude the great metropolises such as London, Paris or Berlin, for they are too vast for the most important group of foreigners attending this or that congress to remain visible); this city, for the duration of a month, would be decked with flags of all nations, she would be alive with the entire variegation of European languages, ceremonies would be held and for decades the city and with her the whole country would have engraved on their collective memory their role as capital of Europe, a role which would bring them to the attention and knowledge of the rest of the world. We should not doubt that these festivities might take on a theatrical air; but, on the other hand, let us remember that nothing is more vital to our somewhat abstract idea than what Germany might term regalia, and France *mise en scène*, and let us beware our indigenous timidity in this regard. Since antiquity all political forms have regularly sought to acquire visibility, and any European politics today must be underpinned by all the powers and stratagems of current European technology, through the radio and loudspeakers, through sporting festivities and performances, through the summoning of huge living crowds, for only a visible crowd makes any impression on the masses and any powerful movement in real space stimulates intellectual activity. If we then travel from city to city we can hope that, in all the places where the various classes of society have been assembled in the manner of a European parliament, these links will remain a vigorous and fertile idea, that the community we have founded in these places will not form an ephemeral closed circle of elites but will be nourished by and reinforced in all classes and all milieux. Thus we might hope that little by little our ideas will gain in popularity. Each city and each country will forge links with others, and that competition which so often translates into hostility we would steer into an amicable rivalry of hospitable communal spirit. Of course, it will be years before our peregrinations spread throughout Europe, but these detours from city to city seem to me more fruitful than the mere use of the word and writing, for these—and let us be quite honest with ourselves here—only ever managed to touch an elevated group that has little weight to bear; but the great masses, those we need to reckon with, they can only be reached through what is placed right before their eyes, through the physically perceivable image, not through the spoken word. They can only be persuaded, in fact, through the most thorough, purposeful organization.

The national sensibility of the French, the Germans, the Italians and all peoples was forged over time thanks to the interaction of the multiplicity of feelings belonging to the native peoples of certain territories. If several centuries were necessary to arrive at that point, we can realistically predict it will take decades for the realization of our idea. The most important thing is to make a start. The advantage, moreover, would be to make clear publicly which European nations are today already ripe for this conception of Europe and which view it with mistrust, or even reject it outright. But I nourish the hope that all will voluntarily welcome without scepticism such a universal congress of nations, and even that a certain rivalry will moreover encourage different nations and cities to want to become the next congress city and capital of Europe.

This will be, I am fully aware, only a beginning. But it will at least provide a way of making our idea visible, more conspicuous, and does not exclude other more effective forms of action which, as long as they remain apolitical and do not entail any commitment, are I hope realistic. The plan I propose might not necessarily be one through which we will progress, but we should I sense at least get something started in some form. Let us not lose any more time, for time is not working in our favour. We can have precious little confidence in such a period of absurdity, where common sense can no longer be relied on. Let us now abandon the aloof humanist way of thinking, the airy notion that with mere words, writings and yet more conferences one can make an impact on a world saturated with weaponry and bloated with mutual distrust. Keep in mind the words of Faust, who firmly rejected the decisive statement "In the beginning was the word" and replaced it with something a little more truthful: "In the beginning was action!"

1914 AND TODAY

I F ROGER MARTIN DU GARD's last novel, *L'Été 1914*, made a greater impression on me than any other book in recent years, I realize that this is not solely due to its extraordinary artistic merit. Martin du Gard's book also has a disconcerting bearing on the present, despite the event it describes having taken place almost a quarter of a century ago. For the atmosphere of those days, which he renders with such convincing intellectual truth, on the one hand reveals a troubling resemblance to the present time, and yet on the other is strikingly different, so that on every page we can't help but compare the situation then with that of today. Our generation, which knew both these times, will be led unceasingly to such a contradiction, and this—along with the moral, documentary and other values the work undoubtedly possesses—can only serve to strengthen its sense of responsibility and moral vitality.

L'Été 1914 is the last volume, the seventh, of the series entitled *Les Thibault*. We remember the first, which tells the story of a family, the school years of two brothers, the fate of a friendship, the conflicts and tensions in a family, a succession of episodes both moving and humane. We were already familiar with the lead players, almost as if they were friends, when abruptly the novel ground to a halt at the sixth volume: *La Mort du père*. Mutterings in literary circles back then were that Martin du Gard had destroyed the manuscript of the original seventh volume, to be called *L'Appareillage*, abandoning any further progress. In fact for years after no further writing appeared and one had the distinct feeling that some obstacle prevented the author from completing his work. But it now turns out that this hiatus was merely a hesitation before the final decisive ascent, for with the rewritten final volume now called *L'Été 1914*, and appearing in two parts, the novel suddenly reached a height from which it presided over all contemporary literature. The lonely destiny of the hero Jacques Thibault, the events in this family's private life led inexorably to the most unambiguous facts of our epoch. The six fatal weeks between the assassination of Franz Ferdinand, heir to the Austrian throne, and the outbreak of war are viewed day by day through their chronological and moral succession in a more majestic and penetrating manner than any historical account could ever muster. This is not a war novel per se, but much more: a novel about the triggering of war. Once again we breathe the same oppressive atmosphere, feel the same emotions, in the feverish anxiety of these fateful days. You confront your memories of that time, in the light of a far clearer knowledge, purer, and naturally you are led to compare the onset of the last war with that of the war which now menaces us. We realize with horror the analogy of the situation then with now and, with still greater horror, the contrast between yesterday and today.

Permit one who has lived through 1914 and who is obliged to relive the dangers of a new war speedily to define this contrast. In 1914—and Martin du Gard recounts this magnificently—war had become something distant, an outmoded phenomenon which no one really believed in nor had any clear idea about. There may have been in Podolie and elsewhere, farther south in the Balkans, a handful of old hunters who had stalked bears in their youth, for even in 1914 there still existed generals and veterans from the campaigns of 1866 and 1870, hoary, gouty old men who had taken part in a European war and tended to reminisce about it. But for the great mass of the population, armed conflict between the powers had seemed for so long something unimaginable, unworthy of such a time of progress and, ultimately, something impossible in the twentieth century. No one dared espouse such a thing openly, and only the closed circles who in their heart of hearts desired it were shamelessly confessing to this desire and making ready. The emperors, chancellors, diplomats and even the officers spoke only of peace and again peace. There were no teachers, politicians or café strategists celebrating war as a necessary "bath of steel", those who made plots merely concealed them from the people. The minority who thirsted for war knew perfectly well that it was necessary to surprise the people through a combination of speed and stratagem, and with artful cunning merely position them before a fait accompli; for not all nations were unanimous in their rejection of war and the clandestine anti-war forces in the twentieth century were always open to dangerous firebrands. In 1914 governments had to face a wave of resistance of a kind, which simply did not exist in 1866 or 1870. During this half-century the Socialist International had been formed, a community of some twenty or thirty million men in Europe whose convictions told them to sabotage any attempt to force a war. Furthermore, in the bourgeois milieux there existed powerful organizations absolutely opposed to war. Bertha von Suttner had begun to organize her pacifist propaganda campaign and numerous politicians, artists and intellectuals lent their support. In 1913 influential groups of German and French parliamentarians made candid visits. And an even more important difference! The entire European press, with the exception of Russia, was by now completely free, a channel for public opinion, which was entirely opposed to war. The pacifist forces then enjoyed total freedom of action, hundreds of thousands of workers—this too Martin du Gard's novel ably recalls—could, till the eleventh hour, still demonstrate in the streets of Berlin and Paris; in retrospect one could say today that a few dozen leading parliamentarians who were energetically opposed to war and the machinations to bring it about could have feasibly prevented the ensuing misery of millions of men. There were in 1914 (and it is vital to stress this) colossal public forces whose action was impossible to predict and who could become dangerous if there were any talk of mobilization. That is why the emperors, kings and presidents did not know, until the very last moment, if the parliaments were approving or not the commendation to go to war, if the millions of workers would let themselves be mobilized, if international social democracy would not trigger a general strike at the last moment. And if there had been in each European nation fifty good men of the like of Jacques Thibault, they would never have allowed this world catastrophe to happen at all.

If it happened in spite of this, the reason is that (today we see it all too clearly) until the last moment no one believed war could actually happen. They thought it an impossibility: the socialist workers had confidence in their leaders who, in the decisive moment, would fearfully abandon their convictions; the bourgeoisie had confidence in parliament, the diplomats; and the diplomats who, for their part, dreaded war and the onerous responsibility that would fall on them, counted on the fear of their counterparts in the opposing country. Austria thought that Serbia would retreat in the face of her threats; Russia believed that Austria would show weakness; Germany hoped that Russia would allow herself to be intimidated, until the crucial moment when, in the ensuing panic and confusion, all nations threw themselves headlong into war with delirious intoxication.

Any such impediment or restraint is completely absent today. Openly and flagrantly, certain countries express their will to expand and make preparations for war. The politics of rearming is pursued in broad daylight and at breakneck speed; every day you read in the papers arguments in favour of armament expansion, the idea that it reduces unemployment and provides a boost to the stock exchange. Whilst in 1914 every intellectual, every politician dared not speak of war or seem to glorify it, today in Europe and in Japan whole peoples are educated and disciplined solely with a view to waging war and with blatant cynicism the whole economic structure of the country is galvanized with this single aim in mind. They await war as if for a perfectly natural event, almost as if of necessity, and that is why the current generation has no excuse to be "surprised" by war as in 1914. For it is laboriously announced, prepared quite openly and lucidly. It is not only at the door, it already has its foot in the house. For those who wish it, this war will be extremely easy to ignite at the moment of their choosing, as easy as turning on the gas tap, for all resistance governments might fear, whether from inside or out, has been snuffed out in advance. There is no longer in Europe anything one might term public opinion. In more than half the countries, freedom of the press has been suppressed and even in those that remain it is under the heel of the various departments of foreign affairs. The idea of internationalism has been scattered to the winds, the League of Nations is shackled and the obligations of treaties and accords cannot be enforced. Once again, those who long for war operate today with an impunity a hundred times greater than their 1914 predecessors because they can deploy their activities openly and without embarrassment, since they are not called on to find moral cover stories to sanction their plans, and above all because they are certain of the impotence and unthinking obedience of their fellow citizens. Of course millions of people in Europe live in fear of war, but the precautions that they are taking against it are of a purely personal order, egoistic. They hoard as much gold as possible and squirrel it away somewhere in a wall, they reinforce their cellars with cement against aerial bombardment, and buy gas masks for themselves and their families. But all have abandoned any notion of collective resistance. There is no longer any pacifist organization to speak of and barely any will to form one. Even the artists and intellectuals are weary of signing manifestos, for they know well enough how absurd it is to wave a scrap of paper at an onrushing locomotive. Faced with the firm and organized resolve of certain leaders and nations to go on a war footing, there is now in Europe—and we should be fully aware of the danger—a situation of total apathy.

Hour of tragedy! The sense of shame of 1914, with its wavering attitude, its inept resistance, but at least a will to resist still in evidence, can now appear to us today like some glorious epoch! Nothing left such a powerful impression on me as when in Argentina I visited the slaughterhouses and saw those beasts down in their enclosure, absorbed in their gentle grazing and lowing (a few pairs were even still indulging in the pleasures of love) whilst on the floor above you saw the flashes, heard the hammering of machines that ten minutes later would kill them, chop, carve, slice, disembowel and dismember them. But then the animal is enveloped by its unconscious; it has no idea to where it is led. Our human herds in Europe, who are today much closer to the butcher than they realize, have no excuse. We must not let ourselves be duped by the fact that they stroll contentedly—no doubt to drug themselves—to the theatre, the cinema, more concerned with the latest fashions and all kinds of other preposterous diversions than facing their actual fate. Deep down they all know the menace that threatens and their dearth of will to confront it. What is so tragic in Martin du Gard's book is that, as he shows in such an admirable way, in 1914 opposition to the war could not prevent catastrophe, whilst any current work which might seek to articulate the intellectual and moral atmosphere of the war facing us will only manage to recount the following lamentable fact: that Europe, in the face of the most extreme danger, could not summon up the least spark of resistance. If we do not finally take hold of ourselves, it will not be another epic saga as in Roger Martin du Gard's book, but merely a sad testimony to the colossal universal fatigue and incomprehensible indifference of the individual today with regard to his own destiny.

THE SECRET
OF ARTISTIC
CREATION

O F ALL THE SECRETS of the world, that of creation has since the beginning been the most mysterious. That is why peoples and religions have always linked the phenomenon of creation to the idea of divinity. For if we can fully grasp and understand what exists as a fact, then each time we will have a sense of the unearthly, the divine, when something suddenly appears where before there was nothing—like the birth of a child, or when under cover of night a flower suddenly bursts out from the bare earth. But where our wonder is greatest, most tending to veneration, and I might say most sacred, is when this newborn thing is not fleeting, when it does not fade away like the flower, does not die like the human being, but survives all time, eternal as sky, earth, sea, sun, moon and stars, whose workings are not of mankind but of the gods.

This perennial amazement that something can be born of nothing and yet defy time sometimes allows us to exist in another sphere: that of art. We know that every year 10,000, 20,000, 50,000 books are churned out. We are well aware that 10,000 paintings are created; a million musical beats composed. None of this is a cause of surprise to us. That writers and poets should write books seems as natural to us as the fact that the books are typeset by type-setters, printed by printers, bound by bookbinders, sold by booksellers. It is the mere phenomenon of production, no different to the baking of bread, the making of shoes or stockings. The first sign of a miracle is when one of these books, one of these canvases, owing to its state of perfection, outlives the epoch in which it was born and then many other epochs. In this case, and only this case, we feel that genius is incarnated in a certain man and that the mystery of creation is reproduced in a work. It's a stirring thought: here is a man made just like any other; he sleeps in a bed, eats at a table, is clothed like the rest of us. We pass him in the street; perhaps we were at school together, sat on the same bench; nothing on the outside suggests that he is any different from us and yet suddenly something happens to this man that is denied to the rest of us. He has broken that law which keeps us all under a spell, he has conquered time; and while we perish, leaving no trace, he endures. And why? Uniquely because he accomplished this divine act of creation where something is born of nothing and that which is ordinarily fleeting in this case happens to persist. Because in his appearance is revealed the most profound secret of our world: the secret of creation.

What has such a man achieved? Take the external. He has, should he be a musician, selected a jumble of notes from the tonal range and grouped them in a particular way to bring forth a melody which has the gift of emotionally resonating with hundreds of thousands of listeners, for ever stirring the souls of millions across the most distant continents. If he is a painter, then with the aid of the seven colours of the spectrum and the alternation of light and shade he creates a painting which, once we have gazed on it, is projected deep into our soul. If he is a poet, he has taken a few hundred words of the 50,000 or 100,000 of which our language is composed, and assembled them in such a way that they constitute an immortal poem. Or if he is a dramatist, a teller through forms, he has created characters who seem so familiar to us that they might as well be brother or friend, people who—like him—possess the divine power to outlast time. Through this external act he has turned the law of nature on its head: he has forged a substance that defies death. Out of a sound in the air he has formed something that moves us deeply, something far more lasting than the wood or stone of this house. In him lies the imperishable and—we can state it with confidence—the divine is revealed through the earthly.

Yet by what means has this solitary being accomplished this marvel? By what means has he and only he among the millions of men, using the same materials available to all, language, colour, sound, created his work of art? What is this secret force with which he is endowed? How does the genuine artist create? How can such a miracle still emerge in a godless world?

I believe all of us have at one time or another asked ourselves this question, either standing before the canvas of an old master, or when a line of poetry touches the deepest recess of our soul, or on listening enrapt to a symphony by Mozart or Beethoven. I think everyone has asked himself or herself with awed astonishment, and precisely because of this astonishment, how a single individual could produce this superhuman work. And I would even venture to say that whoever stands before a work of art and *does not* pose these questions, does not wonder at their secret configuration, has no meaningful relationship with art and never will have. It is the finest element of our human heart to be touched by the greatness and mysteriousness of these works and it is the finest element of the human spirit to unravel this mystery. Whosoever seeks a relationship proper with these works should do so with a double feeling. He must first humbly acknowledge that they exist beyond his own faculty, beyond ephemeral life. But at the same time he must strive with vigorous thought to grasp how this divine inner spark can occur in our earthly domain. He must seek to comprehend the incomprehensible.

Is this possible? Are we really able to monitor the events which precede the birth of a masterpiece? Can we really witness its procreation, its birth? To that I can answer categorically: no. The conception of a work of art is purely an interior process. In every case it remains individual, as enveloped in shadows as the creation of our world—an unobservable phenomenon, an enigma. The only thing we can do is retroactively to reconstruct it, and this only up to a point. But in the end we can only take a step nearer the perplexing labyrinth. We cannot explain the mystery of creation itself, any more than we can explain the phenomena of electricity, gravity and magnetism, contenting ourselves with the establishment of a handful of basic laws. In our search we must conserve the greatest humility and be ever conscious that the act in question occurs in a space inaccessible to us. Even with the most powerful harnessing of our imagination and logic we can only bring to mind the shadowy image of this process, but it is only an image.

We are not permitted to witness the artist at the moment of his creation, but we can try to be in at the afterlife.

To reconstruct this mysterious phenomenon I shall employ a method which at first sight does not seem sympathetic: that of criminology, the practice of which in the last 100 years has developed into a new scientific discipline. In criminology, one must deal with a severe deed or misdeed, murder, thievery; but here on the other hand we are dealing with the noblest acts, the greatest of which humanity is capable. But in essence the task is the same: to illuminate what is hidden, the incident, to reconstruct it precisely using sophisticated and proven methods.

So what is the *ideal* case in criminology? It is when the guilty party—the murderer or thief—stands before the court and explains for what reasons and in what manner, at what moment and in what location, he committed his act. Through such a spontaneous avowal, the police and magistrates are relieved of all effort. In the same way, in our study, the ideal case would be that where the creator himself articulates the whole process, divulging his technique and enabling understanding of that which is incomprehensible to us. If in doing so the poet were explaining how he writes, the musician how he composes and how for each work the inspiration came to him, how the creative idea took form, then that would make all our research superfluous.

But we find ourselves before that strange phenomenon of creators, whether they be poets, musicians or painters, as much as hardened criminals, who are not able to make any definitive statement on that intimate first moment of creation. It is this that Edgar Allan Poe remarks on regarding the evolution of his poem 'The Raven', when he says: "I have often thought how interesting an article might be, written by any author, who would—that is to say, who could—detail, step by step, the process by which any one of his compositions attained the ultimate point of completion. Why such a paper has not been given to the world, I am at a loss to say."

So I ask, if it is not too immodest a question in the case of these great poets, why do we have so few representations by them on the process of their creation? The stock answer given is that they simply did not provide any. The fact that we have so few seems really surprising. For in what consists the gift of a poet or a writer if it is not to tell, to explain? Each journey, each adventure, each inward convulsion is transmitted to us through their books with marvellous force-fulness. It would seem natural then that as a consequence they might furnish precise information, something clear, concerning the way in which inspiration came to them, the rapture and suffering which enabled their labour of creation. Indiscretion, loss of the self, even renunciation of the most intimate being—what the poet professes to undergo—is what makes any first-hand explanation, any declaration of these mysterious states of the soul so vital to us. But if artists speak so little about their moments of inspiration, the reason is that when they are in that moment they are not conscious of the process that is evolving within them; that during the actual creative labour they find it difficult to spy on themselves in any psychological sense, to look over their shoulder while writing. To remain with our criminology example, the artist then resembles the murderer; after having acted in a state of febrile passion, he faithfully states to the magistrate or prosecutor who cross-examines him: "I have no idea why I did it, nor do I remember how I did it. I was not in my right mind."

I know that this *non-presence* of the artist at the moment of creation does not seem at first sight entirely logical. But let us reflect a moment. In reality, creation is only possible in a particular state of *advancing-beyond-self*, a state of ecstasy, a Greek word which, translated literally, signifies nothing more than "to be outside of oneself".

But if the artist really is outside of himself, where is he then? He is in his work, his melodies, his characters, his visions. Whilst creating—and this explains why he cannot be a witness—he is no longer in *our* world, but in *his*. The poet who in a moment of inspiration draws on his memories of a landscape on a spring day, of meadow, sky, tree, field, is not at that moment in his room, within four walls, for now he sees the greenery, breathes the air, hears the wind that sighs over the grass. At the moment when he enters Othello, Shakespeare leaves his own body, his real soul, to penetrate that of an Othello seething with envy. Whilst the artist in that instant of extreme concentration is with all his senses *in the other*, occupying the body of another, absorbed in his work, he is as if closed to all competing impressions from the outside world. To make this state somewhat clearer, I will recall a classic example we learnt at school. At the taking of Syracuse, the ramparts long breached, soldiers were engaged in plundering the town. One of them broke into the house of Archimedes and found him in the garden, absorbed in drawing geometric figures in the sand with a stick. As the soldier advanced towards him sword in hand, Archimedes, deeply engrossed in his work, said without turning around: "Do not disturb my circles." In that divine state of intense concentration he only saw one thing: that someone was going to mess up the figures he had traced. He did not even know it was the foot of a soldier, that enemy forces were in the city, he had not heard the thunderous crash of the battering rams, nor the cries of the fleeing and murdered, nor the jubilation of trumpets. In this moment of creation he was no longer in Syracuse, but in his work. Or let us take another example, from the modern era. A friend pays a visit to Balzac, who appears in state of emotion, tears in his eyes, and welcomes him by announcing the death of the Duchess of Langeais. The visitor is taken aback. He does not know the Duchess of Langeais, or anyone in Paris by that name. But Balzac created this character, whose death he had just described in his book; the artist was so embedded in his visionary world that he had not yet returned to the real one, and it was only on seeing the look of surprise on his friend's face that he came to his senses.

Perhaps these two examples suffice to demonstrate the extraordinary state of complete inner concentration that must accompany any creative act. The true artist is then as occupied by his creation as the believer by his prayer, the dreamer by his dream. As a result, in contemplating the internal, he is unable to see clearly the external, or himself. This is why artists, poets, painters, musicians are incapable, whilst they are creating, of observing themselves, still less of explaining themselves, or by what manner they have produced the work. They are bad witnesses, useless witnesses for the creation courtroom, and, like incautious criminologists, it would be a mistake on our part to rely blindly on their testimony.

What do the police do when the leading witnesses are inadequate or their testimony is flaky? They welcome all information they can find from other sources—and that is what we too must do when we question our contemporaries—for ultimately, to learn anything properly one must visit the scene of the crime, reconstruct it from traces left behind. Let us attempt to do the same.

But where is it then, this place of artistic creation? It does not exist, you will claim. Creation is an invisible process, born of the primary word inspiration—*inspiratio*—which shows clearly that it acts like a breath or *afflatus*, that is to say a purely immaterial phenomenon, one which cannot be registered with eyes or ears, or touch. That is true up to a point. But we live in a terrestrial world and we are people who can only grasp anything with the senses we have at our disposal. For us a flower is not yet a flower when it is enclosed, germinating as a seed in the soil, but only when it evolves into form and colour; a butterfly is only a butterfly when from a caterpillar in a chrysalis it transforms into a winged miracle. For us a melody is only such when we hear it and not when it is heard for the first time in the brain of a musician; a painting is only a painting when it is visible; a thought is only a thought when it is expressed; a form is only a form when it is realized. To pass from the soul of an artist into our life, inspiration is obliged on every occasion to take earthly form, one perceptible to our senses. It must, if I can dare to express it in such a way, pass through a material medium. Even the most sublime poem must, in order to reach us, be rendered with the aid of a material object, pen or pencil, be expressed upon a material object, written on paper or painted with colours on a canvas, or carved in stone or wood. The artistic process—and here we take a step closer—is not pure inspiration, nor merely a process going on behind the brain's wall or passing over the retina, but an act of *transference* from the spiritual to the sensory world, from vision to reality. And because, as I have shown, this act is occurring to a greater extent in sensory material, it leaves behind firm traces that constitute an intermediary state between indeterminate vision and definitive accomplishment. I think of the preliminary works, the draft scores of musicians, the sketches of painters, the multiple versions of poets, of manuscripts, studies, of all the material of formulation now preserved. Since these works left by the artist are silent witnesses, they are more impartial, the only ones we can really trust. Just like the objects left behind by the murderer at the crime scene, the prints he leaves, constitute the most dependable evidence in criminology, so the studies and plans that the artist has left offer the sole possibility of reconstructing the interior process. They are the Ariadne's thread which we can hold on to in the labyrinth which is the creator's brain. If sometimes it's possible at least to approach the secret of creation, we can do it only through its traces.

I say *sometimes* we might approach the secret, for we do not have the self-revealing documents of all the great artists to hand. It's a fatal tragedy that we lack those of the greatest. We have not a single page of Homer, no line from the Bible in its primary form, no Plato, Sophocles or Buddha, nothing of Zeuxis or Apelles. Some of this can be explained by the sheer distance in time, but it seems strange that we have nothing of Chaucer, Shakespeare, Dante, Molière, Cervantes or Confucius; perhaps this is the will of Nature, who wants to say to us: "It is precisely in these great works born of the human spirit that you must possess no earthly knowledge. They must ever remain an inscrutable miracle to you." But there are still other remnants of the geniuses of humanity, from Beethoven and Shelley, Rousseau and Voltaire, Bach and Michelangelo, Walt Whitman and Edgar Allan Poe, whether the houses where they lived or the objects they handled. We also have their manuscripts and their drafts, and whilst we ponder these artists and their work, we can glance indiscreetly into their workshop or studio and get some vague sense of the secret of creation.

Let us try it then. Let us enter a museum, a library, those unique places where one can see objects in which the process of creative production has left a visible trace. Let us reveal the scores of Mozart, of Beethoven and Schubert, the studies of the great painters, the rough drafts of poets, and let us attempt to draw from these witnesses some clarity on what exactly happened during those mysterious hours of creative application, which are at once the most joyful and the most tragic.

First let us hold up a few manuscripts of Mozart, from a purely objective standpoint, and see how the composer worked, first the finished manuscript of a sonata and alongside that the drafts which preceded it, so we might better understand the way in which the definitive work was formed. To our great surprise we learn that there are no sketches and that all we possess are the finished articles, the definitive texts, jotted down in one go in that light, effortless, winged hand. Our first thought when viewing these pages is that these are copied manuscripts. He had someone dictate them and he had them drawn up in a hurry. It's the same with the manuscripts of Haydn and Schubert. In their case we can find no preparatory work and in a general sense no evidence of laborious effort or application. Indeed we know, after the testimony of contemporaries, that Mozart would elaborate his musical themes whilst playing billiards and that Schubert, chatting with his cronies, could select a poem from a book, disappear into the adjoining room, jot down his composition in a notebook and the next thing a song would be born, an immortal one. This ease of composition we see again in the manuscripts of Walter Scott, where over 400 or 500 pages not a single crossing-out, correction or amendment is visible, which further reinforces the sense that this is not a work of composition per se or an act of creation, but rather a transcription under dictation. And then we have certain painters like Frans Hals or Van Gogh, for example—no sketch, no plan. They merely fix their object with a magical eye and immediately the quick and lively brush darts to and fro. They eschew order, assemblage, arrangement. For them creation is all flow, momentum, fluency.

A simple glance over these manuscript pages is sufficient for us to gain a first insight into our secret. The artist when seized by inspiration acquires a higher level of buoyancy. A sleepwalker-like assurance takes possession of him and bears him beyond all those difficulties without steering or guiding his intellect. The creative spirit passes into him and over him just as the air passes into a flute and is transformed into music. The artist is the unconscious medium of a higher will. He himself has nothing more to do than faithfully to execute what this will demands of him, to know how to express purely an inward vision. The state of creation is, then, if we are to believe these manuscripts, a wholly passive state, excluded from all personal human labour.

But let's not pass too rapid a judgement. The process of creation is in reality far more complex, the most mysterious of secrets. Let us then proceed with our researches. And after Mozart's manuscripts, we'll now take a look at those of Beethoven.

This time the impression is quite different. The image offered us concerning Beethoven's creative method seems as in stark a contrast with Mozart's as a Norwegian fjord with an Italian sea. Contrary to what we have just learnt from the Mozart example, where we saw the creative state as a passive one to which the personal will of the artist is excluded, we now discover after that light-footed, winged genius the laborious human struggle, the gradual shaping of man into artist.

Here first are some pages from a notebook of drafts, a few bars scribbled hastily in pencil, almost hurled onto the paper with feverish impatience. Beside them we find bars which appear to bear no relation to those preceding them. Nothing is properly finished; there is no orderly process. It's like a series of rocks some Titan is raining down from on high. Now we know from the testimony of contemporaries how Beethoven composed. He dashed across fields, oblivious to where he was, humming and crooning and singing and beating time with his hands. Now and again he would draw a notebook from the deep pockets of his coat-tails, in which he scribbled with a pencil what had just entered his head. Back home, at his work table, he would resume some of these themes. Now we observe a different kind of sketch, something more serious, written in ink, his first themes. But this is a long way from the fully achieved form. With the stroke of a pen, so violent that it spatters and leaves blots on the paper, he underlines, crosses out and starts all over again. But it's still not quite what he is after. He changes things again, makes corrections. With such fury does he score and strike at the paper that the whole page is torn apart—and one sees here the enraged man at his labours, the man who stamps, groans, curses, because the ideal musical form cannot be expressed from where it originates in his head. It is only after countless drafts like these, each one a field of battle, that the first manuscript is finally written, then the second. And in each of the following, and even in the proofs, he still makes constant changes. Whilst with Mozart the act of creation seems a jubilant, light-hearted act, with Beethoven it is all torture, which brings to mind the convulsions, the agony of a woman in labour. Mozart plays with art as the wind with leaves; Beethoven struggles with himself like Hercules with the 1,000-headed Hydra.

Another example, this time from the world of poetry, shows the direct contrast during the birth of a work, in this case between two distinguished poems of world literature, 'La Marseillaise' and 'The Raven' by Poe. Let us compare their development processes. Rouget de l'Isle is not a poet proper, nor a composer. He was an officer of genius who during the French Revolution found himself in Strasbourg. On 25th April 1792 at midday came the news that the Republic had declared war on the kings of Europe. An atmosphere of drunken exaltation flooded the city. In the evening the mayor laid on a dinner for the officers. During the meal he turned to Rouget de l'Isle, to whom he said: why not write some jubilant verses, and in friendly fashion asked him to compose a song which the troops could sing as they marched into battle. And why not? Until midnight the officers remained assembled, then Rouget de l'Isle set off for home. He had fully participated in the general merriment and had drunk enough; his head rang with toasts and speeches, words such as *"Allons, enfants de la Patrie!"* and *"Le jour de gloire est arrivé"*. He sat at the table and wrote straight out the required lines. Then he took up his violin and struck a melody. In two hours it was finished. The next morning at six, he went to find the mayor and presented him the finished song, the completed composition. Ignoring fatigue, and in a kind of trance, he had somehow created one of the most immortal poems in the world, one of the most immortal melodies, through sheer inspiration. It was not of course he himself who was author, but rather the genius of the hour.

Let us now glance at those few pages where Edgar Allan Poe charts the birth of his famous poem 'The Raven'. How he celebrates himself for having calculated with mathematical precision every effect, every rhyme, every word; how he has, with steely precision and without inspiration, one might say manufactured this poem. Here, a great work was created thanks to an extreme tension of the will, whereas with 'La Marseillaise' there was no conscious plan, and the will did not participate.

So we have already performed our little overture in the doorway leading to the artist's studio. We have seen that in two cases, Mozart and 'La Marseillaise', a work of art can be an act of pure inspiration, where the poet or musician, resembling the Latin "*vates*", the seer or prophet, receives from divinity a message which he transmits to other men without grafting his own labours onto it, and we have seen the contrasting example with Beethoven and Poe—and we might add Balzac, Flaubert and a number of other writers—of the artist who creates a masterpiece through studied work, total application, a conscious effort of thought.

We should not be too surprised at this contrast and remember that in physics one can obtain the same effects with the highest degrees of cold as with the highest degrees of heat. In itself, it is of complete indifference whether the perfect work of art was produced in such and such manner, in the fire of rapture or the icy cold of reflection, by pure inspiration or mundane effort. In reality, with artistic creation, as with nature, the elements are mixed up. There are very few people who are wholly good or wholly evil, only a few who are completely optimistic or pessimistic. What I have tried to show is that there are two extreme poles in artistic creation and what is happening here is in essence a tension between these two poles, whose creative spark is the result. In the same way as in nature the masculine and feminine must unite to procreate, so in the act of artistic creation two elements always come together: unconsciousness and consciousness, inspiration and technique, drunkenness and sobriety. For the artist, production means to *realize*, to transpose from interior to exterior, and bring into our world, through the resistant material of speech, of colour, of sound, an inward vision, a dream image that he saw fully formed in his mind. The artist begins by dreaming his vision, she resides in him and he follows her, in a way he plucks her from the invisible world and bears her into the sensory world. After the vision comes reflection, rather like those Persian warriors who lay out their battle plan in a fog of wine and drunkenness and then next morning with clear heads completely revise it.

If we are going to establish any formula for the process of artistic creation, we should not call it "inspiration *or* work", but "inspiration *plus* work". To create is a constant struggle between the unconscious and the conscious. Without these two elements the creative act cannot happen. They constitute the indispensable foundation; it is within the law of contrast, the final compromise between conscious and unconscious that the artist is imprisoned. Within the limits of this law he remains free. This captivity and freedom the artist experiences you could compare to a game of chess. In a chess game there are likewise two opposing groups, the white and the black. In this case the game is played out on sixty-four squares whereas in the artistic case there are 50,000 or 100,000 words, a veritable rainbow of colours or musical tones. But, like these sixty-four squares which allow countless combinations between white and black, and because no game can ever be exactly the same as another, the process of creation is different for every artist. Perhaps the title of my piece is not quite accurate and it should have been called 'The thousand secrets of artistic creation'. For every artist has, within the limits I have mentioned, his particular secret, each work of art its particular history and we have no other means of explaining them than considering in succession a large number of artists of the most diverse hues. It is only from the sum of these variants that we will gain any clear idea of the creative law common to all.

In fact, if we wished to study all the plausible variations of this process it would take an eternity. What infinite contrasts in space and time, what differences in technique and method! There is Lope de Vega, who writes a drama in three days, whilst Goethe begins his *Faust* at age eighteen and does not complete it until he is eighty-two! There are artists like Johann Sebastian Bach or Haydn who, with the diligence and devotion of an official, compose regularly each day, and then there is Wagner, who either experiences a sudden flash of inspiration or languishes for five years without writing a single note. With one the production flows smoothly like a majestic river; while with the other it's a volcanic eruption. Each creates in distinctive conditions: one can work only in the morning and the other only at night; one has need of external incitement, in the stimulus of alcohol or the indulgence of his surroundings; another by contrast needs bromide to ensure clarity of thought, another still takes opium or nicotine to bring about the dreamy state that encourages visions. One has need of absolute calm to marshal his thoughts; the other can only prepare himself inwardly in bars and cafés, amidst the throng of chatting, laughing people. Each creative man has his peculiarities, his characteristic process that belongs to him and him alone; and as little as one hour of love shares its mystery in common with another, so just as little does one hour of creation. And only he who observes closely can get any idea of the infinite variety of art and life; only he who watches an artist at his labours can know the unique character of his personality. It is not enough to have eaten at his table and chatted with him, to have accompanied him on walks or to have travelled in his company. It is only in the work that his true character is revealed; only in that ultimate secret will we really know a man and a work of art. Goethe, one of the wisest sages of his times, provided a pertinent formula: "We cannot know a work of art only when we see it completed, we must know how it came into being." Only he who has penetrated this *creating* of the artist can have any hope of properly understanding his *creation*.

You may perhaps object: this representation of the method of artistic creation, does it not interfere with the sheer joy of experiencing a work of art? Is it not reckless and indiscreet to lift the veil which conceals the creative artist's powers? Is it not better to stand unknowing before a painting and admire it like a landscape of God, to listen to a symphony without asking in what particular conditions and thanks to what inward labours did such a marvel come to fruition? Is it not preferable to leave the artist's studio door firmly shut, not to pose such questions, and remain silent in gratitude as we cast our gaze over some definitive work? I realize that there is something in this way of seeing things which is seductive, but on the other hand I do not believe in a purely passive enjoyment. I doubt that someone who visits a gallery of paintings for the first time or hears a symphony of Beethoven knows how to appreciate right away the masterpieces they are experiencing. A work of art does not reveal itself at the first glance; like a woman it desires courtship before giving anything more away. To sense fully we must follow on from what the artist sensed. To understand better his intentions we must grasp the difficulties, the resistance that he encountered and was obliged to surmount before he could realize his work. We must recreate his soul in our own—genuine pleasure is never mere passive reception, but an interior coexistence with the work. The aim of my explanations is to show that it is in fact possible, up to certain point, even for the unproductive man to place himself in the creative state of the artist and relive with him the very tensions, the pivotal moments that have accompanied him from the birth to the realization of the work. But we must not make it easy for ourselves as regards this struggle, like Jacob and the Angel, that eternal struggle of the artist who says to the angel of perfection: "I will not let go of you until you have blessed me." We should not abandon ourselves to first impressions, not be too quickly satisfied, for the artist never was with his first plan, his first vision. If we hold in our hands one of the famous engravings by Rembrandt, we think immediately that we have something perfect. But how much our admiration, our knowledge of this magician of shadow and light could still grow, alongside the finished work, if we were to place it alongside the proofs, or rather the sketches and drafts which preceded it! We note that Rembrandt has here toned down a light which is too bright, here deepened a shadow; here a figure is placed farther back where in the first version it was more prominent. From proof to proof the composition emerges as more harmonious, and whilst we view the first as the definitive draft, we now see with the eyes of the artist and realize that a still higher degree of perfection is possible. Instead of embracing with a single glance a landscape as if from the summit of a tower, we see things degree by degree and slowly our eyes become accustomed and more knowledgeable. We learn here to relive the creative act through all its phases, the lesson and vision of the process, as no book, no conference, no science ever can. In the same way as the plastic arts, the poetic arts and composition can also reveal themselves to us if we follow the work of the artist from its most primitive form to its final achievement. We are able to see in a manuscript how the composer or the poet is halted by a phrase or a word. We see him searching for the precise form. One attempt, two attempts, he rejects them. He edges closer to the idea he senses. He starts over again. Finally the dyke is breached, the words flow, the melody takes her limpid course and in us too something flows; the creator has discovered the definitive form and we have found it with him. We have participated in the creation of the work and assisted its birth.

To allow the greatest number possible to experience this rare pleasure, it would be something, to my mind, if the museums would display not only the finished article but the preparatory studies, the sketches, the plans which preceded them, so that people did not regard the finished work as something which just dropped out of the sky, but instead realized that these masterpieces were created by their brothers, men just like them, created through great pain, with suffering, with joy, torn from the raw material of life at the highest price to the soul. The beauty of the stars, the majesty of the sky are not diminished just because we try to search for laws to explain this unfathomable space, to measure the distances which separate us and to calculate the speed with which those silvery beams of starlight reach our eyes. Knowledge does not diminish true enthusiasm; on the contrary, it can only increase and reinforce it. So I hope that, without irreverence, we will in our searching draw closer to the secret of artistic creation, that unique moment where the transient terrestrial limits common to our kind disappear and the immortal begins.

THE
HISTORIOGRAPHY
OF TOMORROW

H OWEVER AT ODDS our opinions might be, there is one fact on which we all agree wherever we may dwell on this earth: that presently our world finds itself in an extraordinary situation, in the midst of a deep moral crisis. In the case of Europe particularly, one has the sense that all its peoples and nations are currently locked in a state of unhealthy nervous tension. The merest inducement is sufficient to provoke a surge of emotion. We welcome bad news far more easily than good. Individuals as much as races, classes as much as states appear more disposed to hate than to listen to one another. No one it seems has any faith in calm and rational processes. On the contrary, the whole world lives in fear that a massive eruption of some kind will occur at any moment.

So what are the origins of this state of angst? I believe it is a leftover of the war, a residue of bacteria resisting in the blood. Let us not forget: the war years in all countries accustomed people to living at a higher and more intense level of feeling. Wars cannot be conducted coolly, coldly. There has to be a tremendous outpouring of passion in order to prolong a war of four years to its bitter end. Without respite they must arouse feelings of hate, anger, fury, passion, and we might here recall Goethe: "Inspiration is not a herring, which can be pickled for many years." Hate, anger, bellicosity are brief-lived emotions and that is why they invented this terrible science known as propaganda in order artificially to prolong these emotional states. Millions of indifferent, peaceful, ordinary people, perhaps three or four hundred million—no one knows the true figure—became accustomed to producing and consuming more hate and hostility than was possible under normal circumstances. Then came peace and immediately they brought a halt to this obligatory hatred and murder, as if simply turning off a gas tap. That too is altogether extraordinary. When an organism is accustomed to drugs and stimulants—coffee, morphine or nicotine—it cannot suddenly be deprived of them, and that is why the need for militarization, for hatred, for combat, has continued to reveal itself in this generation. Only the object has changed. We no longer hate the same enemy. But we continue to hate with the same dangerous passion. It has become a hatred of regime for regime, party for party, class for class, race for race, ideology for ideology. But fundamentally the forms are still those of 1914, determined by the need to establish groups to oppose other groups. In the midst of this so-called peace, our world is dominated by a deep-seated war mentality.

How can we bring an end to this menacing situation? How can we bring down this relentless fever, humanize the atmosphere again, purify an organism blighted by hate, alleviate this moral depression which oppresses the world like a thundercloud? There lies the crucial problem we face, and I do not pretend to have heard of a definitive solution; nor have I come with any proposal for one. I know, we all know, what has happened, and so we especially welcome the American democracy and its government repeatedly reiterating the need for a genuine peace and a lasting entente between peoples. But we have also become rather mistrustful of all these conferences, proclamations and demonstrations. They might have momentarily prevented or shifted from view the maleficent deeds being committed, but they have not managed to transform the moral condition, or rather the immoral, in which the world finds itself. It seems that the calm, reflective voice of reason is just too weak in the face of the loudspeakers that propaganda uses to bark its commands, and moreover it is the nature of reason not to produce immediately noticeable results. What distinguishes the bestial impulse is that it is always concerned with the long term, and therefore we should perhaps divest ourselves of the current generation, that of 1914–18, which wields power in the majority of countries, due to its perennial taste for violence and hatred, its war mentality and glorification of might. Perhaps our own true calling is to focus our strengths on the youth, so that at least the young people of today might be protected from this contagion, this fever. Adults cannot be taught much more: they never seem to learn from bad experiences, and that is why our efforts must be to reach out to the younger generation, whose clay can still be shaped by the hand of the educator. To improve the state of this coming generation and above all to make its lot happier than our own, which in the midst of life was suddenly imperilled by war and practically had its heart ripped apart, we must ensure it is better educated and more humane. And what seems to me most crucial here is to elaborate a new form, a new conception of history rather than the one drummed into us at school. A history that shows the development of humanity, that of their individual country and its neighbours, would help a young person better construct their future image of the world. Nothing has a more profound effect on their moral standpoint as regards life, than the way in which they have learnt and understood history.

So how did we teach ourselves this in school? I must confess that I had all but forgotten. But recently, when I was moving home, my history textbook from the time I was at high school happened to fall into my hands; and you know perhaps we were a little too hasty in setting aside our old schoolbooks, for nothing shows more clearly how rapidly conceptions and viewpoints can change over time. It was there in the old, well-thumbed, dog-eared textbook that I was able to review over such a distance of time the kind of history which had informed our generation. I began to read and immediately I shuddered with horror. The way they had presented the history of the world to such unsophisticated, unquestioning young men! So fallacious, so counterfactual, so premeditated! And instantly it dawned on me—that here history had been artfully prepared, deformed, coloured, falsified, and all with clear, deliberate intention. It was obvious that this book, printed in Austria and destined for Austrian schools, must have rooted in the minds of young men the idea that the spirit of the world and its thousand outpourings had only one objective in mind: the greatness of Austria and its empire. But twelve hours by rail from Vienna—a couple of hours today by plane—in France or Italy, the school textbooks were prepared with the directly opposing scenario: God or the spirit of history laboured solely for the Italian or French motherland. Already, before our eyes had barely opened, we were forced to don different-coloured spectacles, according to the country, to prevent us during our entry into the world from seeing with free and humane eyes, ensuring we viewed everything through the narrow aperture of national interest. From this period came what we call today national German education, the uniformity of minds commanded by a single central power. History, which ordinarily signified the highest objectivity, was force-fed into us with the sole aim of making us fine patriots, future soldiers, obedient citizens. We had to show ourselves humble before our own state and its institutions, mistrustful of other countries and races, and we had to agree with the carefully inculcated conviction that out country was better than all the other countries, our soldiers were better than their soldiers, our generals were more courageous than their generals; that our people throughout history had always been in the right and whatever might happen we would always be right: my country, right or wrong.

So there it was, the first specious orientation that we received from our schoolbooks. And then another example, which I came upon soon enough reading on from the first page to the last of this old book, but no longer with the accepting, naive eyes of the erstwhile youth. So what facts then were engraved on our callow minds? It was arranged in such a way that the most important dates were printed boldly in the margin like so many milestones along a highway, and these dates we had to learn by heart. What were the notable events that were underscored? The vast majority were battles and wars. We had to know in what year BC the Battle of Salamis had taken place and in what year the Battle of Cannae, how long the first Punic War had lasted and how long the second, and so it went on down the centuries, battle after battle, war after war, right up to Trafalgar, Waterloo and Sedan. As for the dates of the First World War, it was for us to know them in a far more personal and deeply felt manner than mere words on the page.

What then of the other events that had occurred over three millennia, thanks to which mankind had passed from cave-dwelling to modern civilization? The old book told not a word of this, nothing of the emperors and kings, the great statesmen and presidents who had, through quiet, guarded labour, preserved peace at any cost in order to safeguard their people and ensure fruitful progress. Instead only Hannibal, Scipio, Attila, Napoleon were deemed worthy of interest, only those men who had led wars were presented as heroes. Right from adolescence the idea was planted in our malleable minds that the most significant thing in the world was war, that war was not only permissible but desirable, as the greatest of exploits it profited the homeland and therefore the most important duty for any man or country was to gain victory, whatever this took, whatever the price—10,000, 100,000, a million men. Well we have now seen where this has led us and we foresee the sequel in this current state of turbulent unrest, demonstrations and upheaval which so troubles our world today.

History teaches us that world war will, in a plethora of ways and with infinite pairs of those guileless spectacles smashed, hoodwink our unsuspecting youth, and now it is on the threshold of starting the whole process over again. This is why I say again how shocking it is to read with new eyes this old tattered schoolbook. For what does it mean when history is only taught as a history of war? It is deeply pessimistic and depressing. One army triumphs over another, one general over another, a people over another; fortresses are conquered; countries become greater or smaller through the annexations of provinces. Is there anything more soul-destroying than this never-ending calendar announcing all the wars of humankind? It is as if in a history book they want to reel off all the football matches played in the last fifty years, at what point Tom beat Jack, or Jack beat Tom. Through four millennia, men have plundered, warred, robbed, enslaved each other, as if mankind has made no civilized progress at all but rather his senses are forever clouded by bloodlust. Or is it more true to say that the only genuine progress made since the battles of Xerxes up to those of Ludendorff is that they no longer kill with a battleaxe, man pitted against man, but mow each other down in ranks with a machine gun? That they no longer pour burning oil from the ramparts of a besieged citadel, but rather rush in the wonderful invention of the flamethrower in order to burn men alive? That now, though drawing on the same old instincts, they simply have more efficient instruments at their disposal? That instead of the minor struggles of the cannibalistic hordes of yesteryear, there are now millions of men facing each other? That one no longer hears the hoarse cries of the old war chiefs, but rather the insidious voice of today's propaganda, its commands barking through the radio or the gramophone? I must confess that, like the old school-book, I find nothing there that might uplift the spirit of a young person of today, that gives a sense of humanity, but only the dread evidence of our endless falling-back into the old barbarism. I could barely restrain my anger, for I saw so clearly how this generation had been brought up to glorify war. The textbook said it all; here were the seeds of those dangerous and evil instincts that have served to poison our epoch.

But in all European states we have been taught the same version of history. And today we see the result. It is forever being shouted down our ears, hammered into our hearts, that victory is the supreme honour, that one man stands for the whole people, and that we remain indifferent to the method by which victory is achieved. Indifferent too, concerning the price paid for this victory—10,000, 100,000, a million men. Instead of moral opinion changing after the war and such acts being viewed as entirely criminal, we witness today with horror that they return to infect the youth in the majority of European countries with an even more terrifying intensity and aura of unbridled extrem-ism. In these countries today people are forced to hear the voices of dictators vaunting the heroic life, declaring that any love of peace is weakness and that there is nothing of greater importance for a man than to die for his father-land on the field of battle. The law codifies this: whatever is for the good of the people is permitted, and ideologies are invented to excuse those actions. Today in Europe we have a systematic deification of lying in the explicit form of propaganda, more powerful than anything known in 3,000 years of history. We bear witness to an exaltation of war as the highest achievement of the soul, one that even the Spartans or barbaric hordes could not dare to match. We are experiencing a falsehood of history that goes right to the heart of our national soul. With our blood seething in our veins, we can only tremble at the thought that, due to this kind of skewed education, the innocent and credulous new generation of young people might be heading for an even more appalling bloodbath than the last.

What can be done about this? Remove history from the school syllabus altogether? No, of course not, for of all human experiences, intellectual development is surely the most essential. So then should we suppress all mention of war in our school textbooks? No, for this would be a falsification of facts and the history of tomorrow must always show the greatest objectivity. But we should demand that what is written harbours a new-found sensitivity, where the spiritual life of humankind is not shown as something stagnating but as progressive, advancing towards the humane and the universal, emphasizing everything that has contributed to this great work of civilization.

This new history we demand must be written with a view to the existing level of culture and the progress to come, rather than that of yesterday, which concentrated uniquely on nationalism and war. For let us remember how our history was born, from Tacitus and Xenophon to the chroniclers of the Middle Ages and on to the modern age.

In that distant epoch the world was not yet a uniform bloc; each dwelt in the narrow framework of their little country; one thinks here of Greece, difficult to locate even on a large map. Men's horizons rarely reached beyond the limits of their own country's borders and they remained ignorant of what was happening elsewhere. But we today live in a world of synchronization, of simultaneous happenings, we know at each second what is going on everywhere, even in the remotest corner of the globe, and we learn about it through speech, through sound and through image. If men lived then as if in the folds of a mountain, their sight limited by the peaks on either side, we today see as if from a summit all worldly happenings in the same moment, in their exact dimensions and proportions. And because we have this commanding view across the surface of the earth, we must now usher in new standards. It's no longer a case of which country must be placed ahead of another at their expense, but how to accomplish universal movement, progress, civilization. The history of tomorrow must be a history of all humanity and the conflicts between individual countries must be seen as redundant alongside the common good of the community. History must then be transformed from the current woeful state to a completely new position; from now on we must say no when yesterday they said yes, and yes when yesterday they said no. In order to have a starting point for its own evaluation, it must clearly contrast the old ideal of victory with the new one of unity and the old glorification of war with a new contempt for it.

Can this be achieved without force? I believe it can. Simply by reversing the signs we can serve truth and morality, for we can recount the history of wars without changing a single fact. Let me give an example. Of all the great representations of war, the most impressive to me seems that of Tolstoy's *War and Peace*. No historian has recounted with more cogent and expressive power the three campaigns of Napoleon against Russia. You live every page. You see the generals and the diplomats bent over their papers and maps, the armies marching, the officers, the soldiers at particular moments of the battle. You are driven along, shaken up, you feel a thousand times more powerfully the momentousness of the event than any war glorifier could muster. But how did Tolstoy retain this sense of movement, of momentousness, this sense of grandeur that he inwardly regards as immoral, and not inspire others to act likewise?

From the opening page he writes: "On the 24th of June the armies of Western Europe breached the Russian frontier and war broke out. That is to say, an event occurred which was at odds with human nature. Millions of men began to commit the most depraved acts—trickery, treason, larceny, plunder, arson and murder—so many that they would have filled every courtroom on earth for centuries. But at that time the men committing these crimes saw nothing criminal about them."

Thus Tolstoy begins his incomparable description of the Russian campaign, and perhaps you may understand more clearly now what I was saying earlier about reversing the signs. During this whole account Tolstoy comments relentlessly on how the absurdity of the event is revealed in every detail. How the brilliant campaign plans both of Napoleon and Kutuzov were never properly executed, how chance steers wars a hundred times more than calculation, how the inferior officers had decorations heaped on them while the more capable were forgotten. Page after page he shows that half of what we hear about wars is a tissue of lies, only a partial explanation of the facts, and we should not attribute any merit to the generals and diplomats, because their acts always take place within the framework of an event which is in itself an absurdity and their accomplishments depend more on luck than on any creative inspiration. We must, then, Tolstoy warns, save our admiration for something more worthy of it than these most foolish exploits, which should only arouse our mistrust.

I think that the history of tomorrow, if it is to fulfil its pedagogic mission, must be written in such a way that wars will not be removed from the schoolbooks but they should no longer be seen as the greatest and most positive exploits of a people. But that is not sufficient. If we view the military actions which break out interminably down the centuries as the dark side of history, there should necessarily be a bright one. I believe that for the three millennia we can embrace with our thought, there has been considerably more going on than just hatred and reciprocal murder between peoples, something else which has encouraged man to leave his cave and learn not only how to kill animals and his own kind, but also to master the elements, gradually to extend himself across the land and on the water, infinitely multiply the strength of his arms through the machine; leading him to invent printing, or allowing him to see things once thought invisible with the aid of the microscope, to study the stars, to calculate their movement in space, to leash the lightning bolt, to speak, to think, to see beyond the continents and the oceans. This conquest of civilization, this intellectual dominance of the world, is it not more important than all those conquests of cities and countries? Is it not the one thing that reassures us that we are slowly succeeding—terribly slowly, admittedly—that humanity is not remaining static, but is advancing towards an invisible objective? And this history of our progress, of our relentless ascension to an ever more noble state of humanity, is it not a thousand times more consoling, more inspiring, for the young and for us all than the bloody roll call of battles and massacres? For does it not tell, instead of the triumph of a single people, a single nation, of our communal triumph, the only one really worth anything?

But it's true; of this communal progress of humanity we have learnt little in our patriotic books. They do not ask that we direct our ambition, our pride towards becoming cosmopolitans, a fraternity, with brotherly feelings; no, these history books tell us to love only our own country—Austria, France or England—and to mistrust other peoples. That is why they insist on nations pitting themselves one against the other, unthinkingly rejecting anything they might have in common. In Europe our history of yesterday, and sadly that of today, follows this same well-trod path of isolationism. It moves in a centripetal sense, where everything that happens and has happened in the world does so through the eyes of the individual state. In the current predominance of nationalism we think from the point of view of the state, whose aim is to force us to think only of the state.

Unconsciously, and I fear even consciously, history itself is placed in the service of the state with equal servitude to that of its citizens.

Now it is my conviction that whosoever sees in this hypertrophy of the state and nationalism the misfortune of our generation and the future one, will contribute to seeing the world released from this hypnosis; and this history of tomorrow, can it not glorify one nation or another but all humanity? We have to change this way of thinking if we wish to see the world raise itself a few steps higher, as when in a landscape the detail becomes lost to the gain of the wider panorama. Such a transformation seems to me not only desirable but also rich in insights. I still remember the revelation I experienced many years ago, from a book which completely overturned the conception of history in our young souls. It was a work by Prince Kropotkin called *Mutual Aid: A Factor of Evolution*. They had been telling us in a thousand books until then that the primordial law of the jungle was the "struggle for existence", and that the forests, the grasslands, the swamps and the sea, the ether and the caves were solely a location for savage struggle and pitiless butchery; one beast hunted down another with the same fury, almost in the same refined way in which men struggled against each other; everywhere the stronger threw themselves on the weak, mutual destruction was the only instinct which appeared to interest the animal kingdom. Now this book by Kropotkin showed, by drawing on a wealth of examples, that precisely in the animal world, which we consider bestial and devoid of reason, mutual assistance in fact existed, not only in one species but between species, that the animal shared man's altruistic instinct and, like him, found it acting in opposition to his egoism. Now, if already by instinct the animals, without even being conscious of it, could act in this way, then surely we who are endowed with a consciousness, the mysterious voice of God breathing through us, can we not overcome our bad instincts? And have we not already been doing that across millennia? Instead of the wars and battles that history cites so frequently, has *this* not been our true strength, that in the past we were cajoled into wars without jubilation and with a bad conscience, and that in spite of all official idealization as practised today, in Germany above all, we always felt mistrustful at heart towards this war heroism? Are we not a thousand times prouder of what our culture has achieved, the progress of our civilization, and should we now present a version of history that suits us better than one which makes us recount forgotten victories, a version that places at the centre of our lives an enriching and encouraging sentiment? We are continually progressing; each decade, each year brings us more inventions, new discoveries, we gain more power over the elements, and even if from time to time we may stumble and fall back for a bloody hour into the old barbarism, we do not turn full circle, we go on unswervingly towards that invisible target.

I believe that if we could endow the history of tomorrow with this certitude that the idea that drove people against people was erroneous and that the only important thing is to push forwards under the banner of a community of nations, the mentality of mankind, that is to say what is

civilized and progressive, would be healthier, more optimistic. Let us compare the history of yesterday with that
of tomorrow from the point of view of moral impulsion.
What does this war history teach us? Only what evil peoples
and countries have wreaked on each other for 3,000 years.
How France plundered Germany and Germany France,
how Persia submitted to Greece and Greece to Persia. And
what conclusion might we draw? That people hate each
other and yearn to go to war. The history of culture, on the
other hand, describes the polar opposite. It does not show
the evil to which one people subjects another, but what
one people owes to another. It shows that almost everything we have invented, thought, dreamt, discovered, is a
collective work, that all invention or discovery was already
gestating somewhere else and was necessarily passing from
one country to another, and that knowing who conquered
and who was conquered was of no concern when the
conqueror was learning something from the conquered
and that in the end all peoples collaborated on building
the Tower of Babel. Whilst the history of yesterday, that
of the wars, relentlessly drives on the young to admire
power as the pre-eminent law and success as the clearest
proof of superiority, the history of culture will teach us to
honour the spirit in multiple forms, this immortal spirit
of humanity, which dictatorship and censorship may gag
for a time but can never entirely snuff out. No longer will
it be the Alexanders, the Napoleons and the Attilas who
are the heroes, but those who served the spirit, who gave
it new form and new expression, those who gathered our
accrued communal knowledge and granted our earthly

senses power over events and clearer understanding of so many secrets of the sky and earth.

But perhaps you will object that placing our history solely in the domain of the spirit, of the intellect and of progress is never going to excite the imagination in the same way as wars, revolutions and audacious expeditions. This objection is quite justified. In our youth we were all more readily inspired by Alcibiades and Alexander, by the heroes of Thermopylae than by the just Solon and the wise Marcus Aurelius. The description of violent passions always favours a writer more than those of moral qualities, justice and humanity, which do not act directly on the imagination and lack explicit emotion. I know from experience that it is more difficult and less advantageous to paint the gentle humanity of an Erasmus than to recount the amours of a Casanova, for example, or the prolific rise of a Napoleon. But why always concede to the unconscious desires of the masses, who only crave thrilling, brutal, warlike historical accounts, served up like so many cheap stimulants? Is our duty not then the contrary, since we are so aware of the implicit danger of this penchant for the sensational, to show, instead of war heroism, this other heroism that we consider superior, the great lives of men of knowledge who sacrificed themselves in their laboratories, isolated, impoverished and overlooked? Those of princes, or men of state who resisted war and who, conscious of their responsibilities, threw all their strength into a spirit of conciliation and humanity? Is it not our duty to advance towards a complete overturning of this destructive hero cult and to replace it with reverence for those who died for an idea, replace those who sent thousands, millions of men to their deaths in a personal craving for power or national supremacy? Is that not the real task of the history of tomorrow, precisely because it is such a difficult and thankless task?

What a vibrant sound will issue from this new way of writing history when it demonstrates the eternal unity of the creative spirit, when it proves that a veritable chain stretches across time, from country to country, from people to people, to which each nation and each year adds a new link. When it will show that the three millennia of our conscious humanity have not been solely a bloody gladiatorial game that an intoxicated God designed for amusement, but that in this grandiose drama we are all at one and the same time poets, actors and heroes; when it will be understood there is a genuine sense to this eternal effort of humanity, that it has a labour to accomplish, to which we all, whoever we are, can permit our modest existence to contribute. In the same way that man is never truly alive until he knows his life has meaning, we can only grasp the past if we recognize some meaning there, namely that of progress towards a higher state of humanity.

I think it is in this spirit that the history of tomorrow must be written: that of the development of civilization. Such a thing is proven possible and already there are clear indications that something is happening. Particularly in the last few decades we have seen attempts to present history not merely as a roll call of battles, as a blood-soaked labyrinth, but as a succession of rungs which humanity has climbed, and I consider it an honour for America that it was here that certain pertinent books found the greatest success and the widest distribution. I recall the narrative of Wells, which constitutes the first serious attempt to consider history as the fruitful reciprocity of nations; I recall America's national history, which was not consciously named *History of America* but *The Rise of American Civilization*; and also van Loon's *Tolerance*. And for me it was a subject of particular fascination when a book like the biography of Madame Curie conquered the States, won millions of hearts, for to my eyes it represented exactly the kind destined for the history of tomorrow, the kind which show the heroism of the human soul, an inward conviction, the heroism of the individual spirit in the service of a wider humanity. This last theme, to know what a man has done, not for himself, not only for his country but for all mankind, is the theme that must pervade the history of tomorrow. Of what relevance today are Napoleon's successes on the Italian battlefields against Austria at Arcole and Rivoli? His empire has long crumbled away into the dust of the past, and the Austria that he conquered has even ceased to exist. But in 1797, in that same year of his victory at Rivoli, and in the same region, a scholar, Alessandro Volta, laboured away beside a tiny instrument. A spark glinted from his first battery, producing a power which today determines and transforms our whole way of life, illuminates the very room in which we are now gathered and makes the human voice resonate around the world, a power which keeps our trains running and has created between peoples a veritable network, a community even the most audacious dreams of our ancestors could never have realized. These then are the acts that our new history will record first, not the ephemeral transformations of the geographic map; and none of it will be lacking, this substance, new acts, heroic acts—of this I am convinced—once the bloody barbarism of conflict finally comes to an end. I was struck by a phrase in the preface to an exhibition of scientific achievements I visited recently. It read: "Never since the beginning of the world has humanity discovered and invented so much as in the past year and yet remained so little informed." A shocking phrase, for we are just not properly informed of what great and encouraging things are happening right under our noses, in our own epoch. We latch on to the minor or major successes of prominent politicians, of leaders, the conquest of a piece of earth, as being the history of our time, but in reality it is merely the history of a moment. What really transforms the interior and exterior life of the next generation is being created now in hundreds of laboratories through some minor experiment or complicated calculation that we have no understanding of yet. But to make the hidden comprehensible and encourage it to enter the bloodstream of our time, to pulse through our thought—this seems to me the key task of the history of tomorrow. That is the true work to which we must apply ourselves and that we must pursue unceasingly, so that we progress in the intellectual domain at every moment of our lives, and through our common bond enjoy the yet to be visible successes, remaining safe in the knowledge that the spirit of humanity will eventually reveal triumphs as yet obscured. It is only in this way that we can console ourselves and guard against the insanity of nationalism and dictators who are bent on launching peoples against one another, ever forcing us backwards politically when the natural momentum is to go forwards. Only when we access this new sense of being will we learn the history of tomorrow; only then will it be possible no longer to despair of our epoch and to retain, even if we failed as citizens, the pride to be men of our time. Only then will we be able to face without horror the bloody vortex of history, when we see it as a necessary creative stage for a new and more meaningful future, as preparation for a complete reworking of humanity. If history is to have any meaning it must recognize our mistakes and overcome them. The history of yesterday describes our eternal relapses, whilst that of tomorrow must describe our illimitable ascent, the history of human civilization.

THE VIENNA OF
YESTERDAY

I F I SPEAK TO YOU of the Vienna of yesterday, it is not an obituary or funeral oration that I am giving. We have not yet buried her in our hearts and we refuse to believe that temporary subjugation is synonymous with total surrender. I think of Vienna as one does of brothers or friends who are at the Front. You spent your childhood in their company, you lived many years in their midst, and many golden hours were spent in kind. Now they are far from you and you know they are in danger. It is precisely in these hours of enforced distance that you feel closest to those held most dear. It is in this sense that I speak to you of Vienna, my home city and one of the capitals of our European culture.

You will have learnt in school that Vienna was always the capital of Austria. That is quite right, but the city of Vienna is a good deal older than Austria itself, older than the Hapsburg monarchy and the former and present German Reichs. When Vindobona was founded by the Romans, who, being such experienced founders of cities, had a wonderful eye for geographic locations, nothing existed of what one might call Austria; neither from Tacitus nor from any other Roman historian is there any mention of an Austrian tribe. The Romans then established in this most favourable site on the Danube a *castrum*, a military stronghold, to repel the attacks of the barbarians against their empire. From this day on the historic mission of Vienna was inscribed: to defend a superior culture, namely the Latin one. In the heart of a territory not yet civilized and belonging to no one were laid the Roman foundations from which later would rise the Hofburg of the Hapsburgs. And in a time when the German and Slavonic peoples living along the banks of the Danube still practised a nomadic lifestyle, it was in our Vienna that the wise Marcus Aurelius wrote his immortal *Meditations*, one of the masterpieces of Latin philosophy.

The first literary and cultural document ascribed to Vienna is around 800 years old. This makes it the leading German-speaking city in terms of the age of its intellectual activity, and for those 800 years Vienna has remained faithful to its task, the highest to which any city can aspire: to create culture and defend it. Vienna became established as an outpost of Latin culture just at the fall of the Roman Empire, acting as a bastion for the Roman Catholic Church. Here was found, at a time when the Reformation was destroying the intellectual unity of Europe, the headquarters of the Counter-Reformation. Beneath the walls of Vienna the Turkish invasion had twice been repulsed. And when now in our own time the barbarians have advanced once more, harder and more tenacious than ever, Vienna and little Austria have remained grimly loyal to their European convictions. For five years Vienna resisted with all her strength; it was only when she was abandoned at a decisive moment that this imperial residence, this capital of our old Austrian culture, was reduced to becoming a provincial city of Germany, to whom she never belonged. For despite being a German-speaking city, Vienna never was a city or capital of the German nation. It was instead the capital of a world empire, far beyond the borders of Germany, from east to west and south to north, spreading as far as Belgium, to Venice and Florence, encompassing Bohemia, Hungary and half the Balkans. Her development and history have never been linked to those of the German people and its national frontiers but to the dynasty of the Hapsburgs, the most powerful in Europe; and the more this Hapsburg dynasty flourished the more the grandeur and beauty of this city grew. It was in the Hofburg, its heart, not Munich or Berlin, which at the time were mere provincial cities of little importance, that history was forged over centuries. It was in the Hofburg that the old dream of a united Europe was unceasingly being born; for it was a supranational empire, a "Holy Roman Reich", that the Hapsburgs strove for, not Teutonism's world domination. All these emperors were cosmopolitan in their thoughts, their words and their aspirations. From Spain they learnt protocol, in art they felt closer to Italy and France and through marriage they were bound to all nations of Europe. For two centuries at the Hapsburg court they spoke Spanish, Italian or French rather than German. Moreover, the nobility who gathered around the imperial house were an entirely international set; Hungarian magnates rubbed shoulders with Polish lords, ancient families of Hungarians, Czechs, Italians, Walloons, Tuscans, Brabançons. You would be hard-pressed to find a German name in all these magnificent baroque palaces grouped around that of Eugene of Savoy; these aristocrats married among each other and into the families of foreign nobility. Always fresh foreign blood was flowing from the outside into this cultural milieu, and likewise this constant intermingling affected the nature of the bourgeoisie. From Moravia, Bohemia, the mountainous regions of Tyrol, from Hungary and Italy came artisans and merchants; Slavs, Magyars, Italians, Poles and Jews arrived in greater numbers into the ever-widening circle of the city. Their children and grandchildren spoke German, but their native roots were not entirely effaced. Contrasts gradually lost their sharpness, became blunted from this relentless mixing; all was softer, more engaging, more conciliatory, more complaisant, more gracious—in a word more Austrian, more Viennese.

Composed of so many diverse elements, Vienna was the ideal breeding ground for a communal culture. Foreigner did not mean foe and what came from beyond the borders was not haughtily dismissed as anti-national, non-German, non-Austrian, but sought out and venerated. All outside stimulus was welcomed and this evolved into the characteristic Viennese colour we know so well. This city and its people may like any other have its faults, but Vienna has had the advantage of not being arrogant, of not trying to foist its mores or world-dictatorial mindset on others. The Viennese culture was not a conquering one and this is why each new guest is so easily won over by her. To mix these disparate elements and create this perpetual harmonization has been the true genius of the city. That is why in Vienna there is always the sense of living in a world dominion and not being closed in by any single language, race, nation or idea. At every moment one is reminded of being at the heart of a supranational empire. It's enough to read off the names on the shop signs: one has an Italian tone, a second Czech and a third Hungarian, and there are even special signs stating that French and English are spoken here. A foreigner without German is never lost. Everywhere one feels, through the local national dress worn so freely and openly, the rich-coloured presence of neighbouring countries. You would see the Hungarian Imperial guards with their back-swords and fur trimmings, the nurses from Bohemia in their colourful dresses, the peasants of Transylvania with their blouses and embroidered bonnets, just like those they wore in their village on Sundays when they went to church, Bosnian peddlers in short trousers and red fezzes who went from house to house selling Tschibuk pipes and daggers, the mountain folk with bare knees and feathered hats, the Galician Jews with their curled braids and long kaftans, the Ruthenians with their sheepskins, the vintners in their blue aprons, and at the centre of this world, as a symbol of unity, the multicoloured uniforms of the soldier and the cassocks of the Catholic priest. All wore the national costume of their homeland as if Vienna itself were that homeland. All had the same feeling, that this was their home, their metropolis; they were not foreigners and never considered themselves as such. The old Viennese scoffed at them in a good-humoured fashion, in popular songs there was often a couplet about the Czechs, the Hungarians and the Jews, but it was always a well-meaning mockery, as that between brothers. They never hated, for it was not in the Viennese mentality to do so.

In any case such an idea would have been preposterous; all Viennese had either a grandfather or brother-in-law who was Hungarian, Polish, Czech or Jewish. The officers and functionaries had all spent several years in some garrison town of the provinces; they had all learnt the language, married; that's why the oldest Viennese families always contained children born in Poland, Bohemia or Trentino. In middle-class homes the servants were more often than not Czechs or Hungarians. Also from childhood, all of us knew a few jokes in a foreign tongue; we knew the Hungarian and Slav popular songs that the servants were singing in the kitchen; the Viennese dialect was coloured with foreign terms, which little by little were cemented together with German. From this our German became less hard, less accentuated, less angular, less precise than that spoken by the Germans of the north, ours was softer, more lax, more musical, and this enabled us to master foreign languages better. We experienced no hostility or resistance, it was customary in the higher levels of society to speak in French and Italian, and we absorbed the music from these languages into our own. All in Vienna were nourished by the characteristics of neighbouring peoples. I choose the word "nourish" in the literal material sense, for the famous cuisine of Vienna was a melange of tastes. From Bohemia came the famous desserts, from Hungary came goulash and other delicacies spiced with paprika, from Italy, Salzburg and southern Germany special regional dishes, and all that was intermingled, blended together, so it ended up as an altogether new cuisine: Austrian, Viennese.

As a result of this constant mixing the people and everything else in Vienna were far more easy-going, even-tempered, pleasant, and this conciliatory character, which was a secret of the Viennese soul, could equally be found in Austrian literature. In Grillparzer, our greatest drama-tist, there is the same creative strength as in Schiller, but thankfully without the melodrama. The Viennese is too self-aware to be melodramatic. With Adalbert Stifter the reflective character of Goethe is in some way transmuted into the Austrian, into something softer, more tender, more appealing and picturesque. And Hofmannsthal, part Tyrolean, part Viennese, part Jew, part Italian, shows us in a symbolic way what new values, what finesse and what happy surprises can result from such a melange; in both his poetry and prose is found the highest musicality that the German language has ever attained, a truly harmoni-ous grafting of the German genius with the Latin, which could only occur in Austria, this country located between two cultures. But that has always been Vienna's secret: to welcome, to adopt, to forge links of spiritual conciliation and transform dissonances into harmony.

It is for this reason and not by pure chance that Vienna became the classic city of music. Like Florence, where painting scaled the highest peaks in the joy and glory of gathering to its walls, in the space of a century, all the great creators, Giotto and Cimabue, Donatello and Brunelleschi, Leonardo and Michelangelo, so Vienna gathered to its bosom in the space of a century all the leading names of classical music. Metastasio, the king of opera, settles opposite the Hofburg, Haydn lives in the same house, Gluck gives lessons to the children of Maria Theresa and to Haydn comes Mozart, to Mozart Beethoven and close by are Salieri and Schubert and after them Brahms and Bruckner, Johann Strauss and Lanner, Hugo Wolf and Gustav Mahler. Not a moment's pause in 150 years, not a decade, not a year where in Vienna an immortal work is not born. Never did the god of music bless a city so much as Vienna in the eighteenth and nineteenth centuries.

Some might raise an objection: of all these masters, none save for Schubert was a genuine Viennese. I do not intend to contest this. Certainly Gluck came from Bohemia, Haydn from Hungary, Caldara and Salieri from Italy, Beethoven from the Rhineland, Mozart from Salzburg, Brahms from Hamburg, Bruckner from High Austria, Hugo Wolf from Styria. But why did they all arrive from the four points of the compass to Vienna alone, why did they choose this city in which to practise their art? Because presumably they could earn more money there? On the contrary. Neither Mozart nor Schubert were exactly sitting on a fortune and Haydn earned more in London in a year than he did over the six decades he spent in Austria. The real reason why the musicians settled in Vienna and remained there was the simple fact that they sensed the cultural climate required for the development of their art was more favourable here than anywhere else. In the same way a plant requires a sympathetic soil in order to flourish, so art needs to develop within a receptive sphere, in a widening circle of connoisseurship, and like the plant it needs sun and light, the stimulating warmth of a great empathy. The highest levels of art are always attained where it is the passion of the whole people. If the sculptors and painters of sixteenth-century Italy gathered in Florence, it was not only because there they encountered the Medicis, who offered them money and commissions, but because the entire people placed its pride in the presence of these artists, because every new canvas was an event more significant than any in politics or commerce, and this fact led artists into a constant striving to surpass one another.

The great musicians could hardly find a better city in which to carry out their work than Vienna, for it had the ideal public, because a fanaticism for music had penetrated all levels of society. A love for music inhabited the imperial palace: Emperor Leopold composed himself; Maria Theresa keenly followed the musical education of her children; Mozart and Gluck played in her house; the Emperor Joseph knew every note of the operas he had performed in his theatre. They even neglected politics in favour of music. Their orchestra, their theatre was their true pride, and in the sprawling domain of state administration they never looked as closely at questions as at those that asked: which opera should I have performed, which conductor, which singers should I employ? This was their greatest concern.

In this passion for music, the high aristocracy wants to outdo the imperial house. The names of Esterházy, Lobkowicz, Waldstein, Razumovsky and Kinsky, all immortalized in the biographies of Mozart, Haydn and Beethoven, have their own orchestras or at least a quartet.

All these proud aristocrats, whose houses were never opened to the bourgeoisie, accept the musician's authority. They do not consider him an employee; he is not simply a guest but a guest of honour, and they submit to his vagaries and pretensions. Dozens of times Beethoven has his imperial pupil the Archduke Rudolf wait for his music lesson and the latter never once complains. When Beethoven wants to withdraw his *Fidelio* before the performance, a princess and countess fall to their knees begging him to relent; one can scarcely imagine today what this gesture by people of noble stock represented, prostrating themselves before the son of a drunken provincial pastor. When the Princess Lobkowicz annoys Beethoven, he comes to the door of her palace and bawls before her lackeys, "Lobkowicz you ass!" But the Princess simply tolerates it and does not bear him a grudge. When Beethoven wants to leave Vienna, the aristocrats offer him an annuity sum, enormous for the period, with no other obligation than that he stay on in Vienna and freely devote himself to his art. Though they might have been mediocre in other disciplines, they all know what great music is and how precious and worthy of admiration such a monumental genius. They encourage musicians not through snobbism, but because they dwell within music and place it on a rung far higher than their own.

It is with equal success and passion that in the same epoch musicians mix with the Viennese bourgeoisie. In virtually every house they hold a chamber concert once a week. Every cultivated man plays an instrument; every girl from a good home can sing from an open book and be part of a choir or orchestra. When the bourgeois of

Vienna opens his daily paper, it's not to read what is happening in the world of politics, but what is playing at the
opera or theatre, who were the singers, the conductor, the
players. A new work is an event: the engagement of a new
conductor or opera singer provokes endless debate, and
backstage gossip spreads through the city. For the theatre,
and particularly the Burgtheater, signifies much more for
the Viennese than a mere theatre: it is a microcosm playing within a macrocosm, a sublimely concentrated Vienna
in the interior of the other, a society within a society. The
imperial court theatre shows people how one behaves in
society, how conversation is held in a salon, how one dresses,
how one speaks, how one comports oneself, how one holds
a teacup, how one enters and then takes one's leave. It's
a kind of *Cortegiano*, a morality mirror of good conduct,
for at the Burgtheater as at the Comédie-Française not a
word is out of place, as in the same way at the Opera not
a wrong note is struck: for to do so would be tantamount to
national shame. They attend the Opera, the Burgtheater,
in the Italian style, as if a salon. They greet each other,
they know the faces, they are quite at home. All classes rub
shoulders with each other: the aristocracy, the bourgeoisie
and the new youth. They are the great community, and all,
everything that happens there, belongs to the city. When it
was decided that the old building of the Burgtheater should
be demolished, the place where *The Marriage of Figaro* was
first performed, it was like a day of mourning in Vienna.
From six in the morning enthusiasts queued at the doors
and remained standing there until evening, for thirteen
hours, without food or drink, just so they could attend the

last performance. They tore splinters of wood from the stage, which they piously conserved, as they once had the splinters of the Holy Cross.

Exaggeration, you will say, an absurd exaggeration! And that's what we too think sometimes about this delirious enthusiasm of the Viennese for music and theatre. Yes, I know it is sometimes absurd. For example, when the Viennese plucked hairs from the manes of the horses harnessed to Fanny Elssler's coach; and I know too we have paid dearly for this fanaticism. For while the Viennese were caught up in their unbridled passion for theatre and music, the Germans were overtaking them in the domain of technology, efficiency and the more practical things of existence. But let us not forget: such overvaluing also creates values. Only where true enthusiasm for art exists does the artist feel comfortable, when so much is demanded of art. I believe there is no other city where the musician, the singer, the actor, the conductor, the director are placed under more scrutiny and constrained by a greater tension. There is not only the critique of opening night, but also an unrelenting and entrenched public critique. In Vienna, no mistake is tolerated at any concert; every performance, whether it be the twentieth or hundredth, is subjected to the same degree of lucid and penetrating critique on the part of every spectator or listener. We are accustomed to the highest levels of quality and are not willing to give an inch. This knowledge was forged in us from an early age. When I attended high school, I was one among two dozen of my classmates who never missed a performance at the Burgtheater or the Opera; being the true Viennese we were, we cared nothing for politics or political economics and we would have been ashamed to know anything about sport. Even today I can't make out the difference between cricket and golf and the football reports in the papers might as well be written in Chinese. But at the age of fourteen or fifteen I could discern any slip or cursoriness in a production; and we knew exactly by which means this or that conductor raised the tempo. We were for or against such and such an artist; we either worshipped them or reviled them, we two dozen of our class. Imagine then these two dozen high school students multiplied by fifty schools, plus a university, a bourgeoisie, a whole city, and you may comprehend the level of tension that such an interest in all theatrical and musical works must engender, how much this untiring, relentless scrutiny must have stimulated the overall level of these musical and theatrical works. Every musician, every artist knew that no drop in standards would be tolerated in Vienna, that he had to strive to the maximum if he were to maintain his standing. This scrutiny carried into the lower stratum of the people. The regimental orchestras competed between themselves, and our army possessed—I always remember the debut of Lehár—far better conductors than generals. The little female orchestras in the Prater, the pianists in the cabaret, where they drank new wine, were all placed under this merciless scrutiny, for the quality of the orchestra was for the ordinary Viennese as important as that of the wine; the musician had to play well, otherwise he was lost, he was dismissed.

Yes, it was strange, everywhere in Vienna, in public life and morals, in the city administration, there was a good deal of nonchalance, indifference, mellowness, a sort of "sloppiness", we used to say. But in the sphere of art no negligence was excused, no sluggishness was tolerated. It is possible that in this exaggerated passion for music, theatre, culture, Vienna, the Hapsburgs and Austria as a whole had forfeited political success. But it is this we can thank for our musical empire.

In a city which exists so profoundly in music, with nerves so attuned, with such a subtle sense of rhythm and cadence, dance must, as a gregarious distraction, transform itself into art. The Viennese danced with passion; they were dance-mad and that went for the balls of the royal court and the Opera right down to those performed in the pubs of the suburbs and by rural farm-workers. But they were not content with dancing voluntarily. To dance well was a social obligation, and when they said of an otherwise unremarkable person that he was an excellent dancer, that signified a certain social standing. He was thereby promoted to a sphere of culture, because they had made of dance an art. On the other hand, because dance was considered an art, they raised it to a higher level, and the so-called light music, dance music, became a complete music in itself. The public danced a great deal and did not always want to hear the same old waltzes. The musicians were compelled perpetually to offer up new ones and outdo each other. That's why alongside the greats, Gluck, Haydn, Mozart, Beethoven and Brahms, there evolved a second line of musicians, from Schubert, Lanner, Johann Strauss father and son to Franz Lehár and other greater and lesser masters of the Viennese operetta—an art which wanted to make life lighter, more animated, more colourful, more wanton, an ideal music for the light hearts of the Viennese.

But I realize I run the danger of lending an impression of our Viennese which too easily corresponds with the soft and sentimental tones of the operetta. A frivolous, theatre-mad city which knows only how to dance, sing, eat, love, where no one has any cares or knows what work is. As in any legend, there is more than a germ of truth in this. Certainly we lived well in Vienna, we led an easy life, we strove to pass off with a quip all that was unpleasant or oppressive. We revelled in celebrations and amusements. When the military bands passed by, people stopped whatever they were doing and raced into the streets. When the flower parade took place in the Prater 300,000 people turned out, and even a burial was an excuse for a pageant and celebration. A wind of lightness blew down from the Danube and the Germans looked on us with a kind of mistrust, like children who did not take life seriously enough. For them Vienna was the Falstaff of cities, wanton, wisecracking, jocular, and for Schiller we were Phaeacians, the people for whom it is always Sunday, over whose stoves the spit never stops turning. They all thought that life in Vienna was too frivolous, too casual. They reproached us for our spirit of "*jouissance*" and for two centuries blamed us because we liked the good things in life so much.

I won't deny this spirit of "*jouissance*" among the Viennese and I will even defend it. I believe the good things in life exist so one might profit from them and it is the supreme right of every man to live freely, without anxieties, without longing. I believe that an excess of ambition in the soul of a man, as with a people, destroys precious values and that the old adage of Vienna, "live and let live", is not only humane, but far wiser than all the severe maxims and categorical imperatives. It is on this fact that the Austrians, who have never been imperialists, will never see eye to eye with the Germans, even with the best among them. For the German people the concept of "*jouissance*" is always linked to effort, activity, success, to victory. To be fully himself, each must outstrip his neighbour and if possible oppress him. Even Goethe, whose greatness and sagacity we so admire, raises this dogma in a poem which ever since early childhood I have felt was anti-natural. He says of men:

> You must reign and conquer,
> or be subservient and lose, suffer or triumph,
> be the anvil or the hammer.

Well, I hope you will not accuse me of impertinence if I offer an alternative to "You must reign and conquer". I believe that a man or a people should *neither* reign *nor* conquer. Above all one must be free and leave others to their freedom; as we have learnt in Vienna, one should live and let live and not be ashamed of taking pleasure in existence. "*Jouissance*", it seems to me, is a right and almost a duty of man, as long as it does not wear him down or weaken him. And I have always noted that it is those who, for as long as they were able, freely and frankly took pleasure in life who in the hour of despair or danger showed themselves more robust, in the same way as men and peoples who fight each other not through love of militarism but only when they are forced to do so, prove themselves the most able combatants.

Vienna showed this at the time of its hardest struggle. It showed that it could work and it must work when it mattered and those who had been dismissed as frivolous showed that, when the need arose, they could be impressively earnest and resolved. No city in 1919 had been so brutally struck as Vienna. Imagine, an empire of fifty-four million people suddenly reduced to four million. It is no longer the Emperor's city; the Emperor has been chased out and with him the lustre of festiveness. The arteries leading to the provinces from where the capital drew its resources have been severed; the railways lack coaches, the locomotives coal; the shops are empty, there's no bread, no fruit, no meat, no vegetables and the currency is depreciating hour by hour. Everywhere they prophesy the end for Vienna. Grass grows in the streets, tens, hundreds of thousands of people are forced to leave in order not to die of hunger; they seriously consider selling off the art treasures to pay for bread, and to demolish whole swathes of ruined houses.

But this old city harboured a strength no one had suspected. In fact she had always shown this strength for life, this strength for work. But, unlike the Germans, we did not loudly brag about it; better still, our mask of frivolity had deceived even ourselves of this work which had patiently been accomplished within the arts and the manual crafts. In the same way that foreigners viewed France as the country of profligacy and luxury—failing to see beyond the jewellers' shops on the rue de la Paix and the nightclubs of Montmartre, never having laid eyes on Belleville, never having seen the workers, the bourgeoisie, the provincials in their steady and determined labour—so too they were mistaken about Vienna. Now it was challenged, all was accomplished and no time was wasted. We did not squander our moral strength denying defeat as in Germany, where they declared, "We were not beaten, we were betrayed!" We said honestly, "The war is over, let us get back to work. Let us reconstruct Vienna and Austria!"

And the miracle happened. Within three years everything had been rebuilt, within five years were raised those communal houses which served as a social model for the rest of Europe. The galleries and the gardens were restored; Vienna became more beautiful than ever before. Commerce picked up, the arts flourished, new industries emerged and soon in a hundred different areas we were at the forefront. We had been easy-going and frivolous, living off the old capital; but now all was lost a new energy emerged which surprised us all. To the university of this impoverished city converged students of all countries; around our great master Sigmund Freud a school evolved which in Europe and America had a bearing on all intellectual activity. Whereas in the past we relied on Germany for the publishing industry, now large publishing houses established themselves in Vienna, commissions came from England and America to study the municipal system of social support, the arts and crafts acquired, thanks to their unique qualities and taste, a dominating position. All was suddenly activity and intensity. Max Reinhardt left Berlin and set up the Wiener Theater. Toscanini came from Milan, Bruno Walter from

Munich; and the Vienna Opera, and Salzburg, where all Austria's artistic forces were communally represented, became the international capital of music and an unprecedented triumph. In vain did the chambers of music in Germany strive, with the limited means at their disposal, to turn this tide of foreigners from across the world towards Munich and other cities. But they could not manage it. For we knew why we were struggling; Austria found itself suddenly confronted by a new historic task: to safeguard before the world the freedom of the German language, already enslaved in Germany, to defend our old heritage, European culture. That gave this what you might call carefree city a marvellous strength. Such a feat of resurrection was not the work of a single man or a party, or of Seipel, the Catholic, any more than the social democrats or the monarchists, but everyone, the entire life force of a two-millennia-old city. I can say without any hint of pettifogging patriotism: never had Vienna displayed so gloriously her cultural credentials; never had she earned to such a degree the sympathy of the whole world than an hour before the great assault on her independence.

It was a beautiful and glorious day in her history. This was her final struggle. We were resigned to the loss of all prosperity and assets. We had sacrificed the provinces; no one dreamt of salvaging a scrap of territory from the neighbouring countries of Hungary, Bohemia, Italy or Germany. We might have been poor patriots in the political sense of the term, but there was one thing we would not cede, nor let ourselves be surpassed in: art and the culture we felt to be our true homeland. Also the most glorious page in Vienna's history happens to be the way in which she defended this culture. I can quote an example: I have travelled much, been present at a number of admirable performances, at the Metropolitan Opera under Toscanini, where I have heard the greatest singers, at the ballets of Leningrad and Milan, but I must confess that I have never been so awestruck as by those which occurred at the Vienna Opera following the collapse in 1919. We groped our way through the darkened streets—street lighting restricted by a shortage of coal—paid for a ticket with worthless banknotes, entered the familiar space, to be struck with horror. The room, with its clutch of lamps, was grey and icy-cold: no colour, no radiance, no uniforms, no evening wear. Just a crowd of people huddled together, dressed in worn-out winter coats and uniforms, a grey, livid mass of shadows and spectres. The musicians entered and took up their positions in the orchestra. We knew them all and yet we scarcely recognized them now. Grizzled, wintry, decrepit, they sat there in their tails. We knew that at this time these artists took home less than a waiter or a manual worker. A shudder seized the heart; there was so much impoverishment, so much dejection and misery in that space, one truly felt the breath of Hades. The conductor raised his baton and the music began. Darkness fell and all of a sudden the old sparkle returned. Never had our opera played and sang better than in those days, so much so that they wondered if they would be obliged to bar the doors the next day. None of the singers, none of the wonderful musicians had accepted the numerous more alluring offers made by rival cities, each had felt duty-bound to give the best of himself and to preserve the common good which was most precious to us: our great tradition. The empire had gone, the roads were in a lamentable condition, the houses had the appearance of having just suffered bombardment, the people seemed struck by a grave illness. Everything was neglected and already half lost; but this one thing, art, our honour, our glory, we defended in Vienna, each playing their role. Everyone worked twice, ten times as hard and suddenly we sensed the world was watching us, recognizing us, as we had already recognized ourselves.

That is how, through a fanaticism for art, a passion so often ridiculed, we once more saved Vienna. Expelled from the top rank of nations, we nevertheless conserved our place at the heart of European culture. The mission to defend a higher culture against all forms of barbarism, the mission that the Romans engraved in our very walls, was accomplished right up to the final hour.

We fulfilled our mission in the Vienna of yesterday and we shall continue to fulfil it abroad and everywhere. I spoke of the Vienna of yesterday, the Vienna where I was born and where I lived and which I love today more than ever now that I have lost it. Of today's Vienna (1940) I can say nothing. We know very little of what is happening there; we are even fearful of interpreting it too exactly. I read in the papers that they had summoned Furtwängler to take in hand the musical life of Vienna; surely Furtwängler is a musician whose authority none can contest. But the fact that they have to reorganize the musical life of Vienna shows that the venerable, miraculous organism is mortally threatened. After all, you hardly call for a doctor to visit a man in robust health. Art, like culture, cannot prosper without freedom, and the culture of Vienna cannot flourish if it is severed from the vital source of European civilization. The mighty struggle that today shakes our world will definitively decide the fate of this culture and I hardly need tell you on which side my most fervent wishes stand.

IN THIS
DARK HOUR

AMONG THE EUROPEAN WRITERS gathered here today whose aim is to endorse our old avowal of faith in favour of intellectual union, we have, at least those of us who are writers in German, a painful and tragic prerogative. We were the first to be confronted by the barbarism now terrorizing the world. Our books were the first to be cast onto the pyres. With us began the expulsion of many thousands of people from their homes and their homeland. At the beginning it was a severe test for us. But today we have no regrets over this enforced exile. For how would we be able to look the free countries and ourselves in the eye, if we had spared the Germany of today or even venerated her? Our conscience feels that much more liberated, having made a clean break from those who have plunged this world into the greatest catastrophe in all history. But at the same time, we feel a sense of detachment from any responsibility for the brutal acts committed today in the name of German culture, though the shadow of these acts still weighs peculiarly on our souls. But you, my other European friends, have things rather easier. Faced with these barbaric measures which threaten the very dignity of man, you can at least state with pride: "It has nothing to do with us! This is a foreign spirit, a foreign ideology!" Whilst we German writers, we must bear these violations as a secret and odious shame. For these decrees are issued in the German language, the same one in which we think and write. These brutalities are committed in the name of the same German culture that we have laboured to serve through our works. We can hardly deny that it is our homeland which has foisted these horrors on the world. And although in the eyes of Germans today we are no longer their countrymen, I feel the need here to express an apology to each of my French, English, Belgian, Norwegian, Polish and Dutch friends for all that has befallen their peoples in the name of the German spirit.

Perhaps you are surprised that we continue to create and write in this German language. But if a writer can abandon his country, he cannot wrench himself from the language in which he creates and thinks. It is in this language that we have, throughout our lives, fought against the self-glorification of nationalism and it is the only weapon remaining at our disposal that allows us to continue fighting against the force of nationalist criminality which is laying waste to our world and trampling the spiritual endowment of mankind into the muck.

However, my friends, if we have lost faith in any optimistic outlook following this horrifying plunge of humanity into bestiality, we have still gained something through the enduring trial. I believe that each of us today has been instilled with a new consciousness and is more aware of the necessity and fundamentally sacred character of intellectual freedom than in former times. For it's always that way with the sacred value of life. We forget it as long as it belongs to us, and give it as little attention during the unconcerned hours of our life as we do the stars in the light of day. Darkness must fall before we are aware of the majesty of the stars above our heads. It was necessary for this dark hour to fall, perhaps the darkest in history, to make us realize that freedom is as vital to our soul as breathing to our body. I know—never has the dignity of man been so abased as now, nor peoples so enslaved and maltreated; never has the divine image of the Creator in all His forms been so vilely defiled and martyred—but never, my friends, never ever has humanity been more aware than now that freedom is indispensable to the soul. Never have so many men reviled tyranny and oppression with such unanimity; never have so many men thirsted for a message of redemption than now when their mouths are gagged. If today a single one of our words can penetrate their prisons, those inside will draw courage from the fact that their oppressors have celebrated victory prematurely. For they will know that there are still free men existing in the free countries who not only desire freedom for themselves but for all men, all peoples, all humanity.

And rightly this freedom, which is assured here, in this free country, imposes on all of us, and especially us writers and poets, a sacred duty; never in our life have we known such a critical and defining moment as this. It is for us today, those to whom words are granted, in the midst of a reeling, half-devastated world, to maintain in spite of everything faith in a moral force, confidence in the invincibility of the spirit. Let us then make common cause; let us accomplish our duties in our work and in our life, each in their own mother tongue, each for their own country.

If we can remain faithful to ourselves at this hour and at the same time to one another, then we will at least have performed our duty with honour.

DETAILS OF FIRST
PUBLICATION

'THE SLEEPLESS WORLD'
'Die schlaflose Welt' (1914)

First appeared in the Viennese newspaper *Neue Freie Presse*, 1st August 1914. Included in Zweig's *Begegnungen mit Menschen, Büchern, Städten* (Vienna, Leipzig, Zurich: Herbert Reichner, 1937; Berlin and Frankfurt: Fischer, 1955).

'THE TOWER OF BABEL'
'Der Turm zu Babel' (1916)

First appeared in the April/May 1916 edition of Geneva-based pacifist journal *Le Carmel*, then on 8th May 1916 in the newspaper *Vossische Zeitung*, Berlin.

'HISTORY AS POETESS'
'Die Geschichte als Dichterin' (1931)

First published in the *Neues Wiener Tagblatt* on 22nd November 1931. Extended and amended for PEN conference in Stockholm, September 1939, but never presented due to the outbreak of war that month. First published in the collection *Zeit und Welt. Gesammelte Aufsätze und Vorträge 1904–1940*, ed. Richard Friedenthal (Stockholm: Bermann-Fischer, 1943).

'EUROPEAN THOUGHT IN ITS HISTORICAL DEVELOPMENT'
'Der europäische Gedanke in seiner historischer Entwicklung' (1932)

A lecture given by Stefan Zweig in Florence on 5th May 1932, then repeated in Milan. First published in *Zeit und Welt. Gesammelte Aufsätze und Vorträge 1904–1940*, ed. Richard Friedenthal (Stockholm: Bermann-Fischer, 1943).

'THE UNIFICATION OF EUROPE: A DISCOURSE'
'Einigung Europas. Eine Rede' (1934)

Unfinished manuscript, written around 1934 and finally published in an edition by Tartin Editionen, Salzburg, 2013, edited by Klemens Renoldner. The essay was among the typed documents dating from the period of Zweig's exile in England and bears Lotte Zweig's handwritten note in pencil in the margin: "The Unification of Europe. Lecture for Paris, not given."

'1914 AND TODAY'
'1914 und heute' (1936)

Written in celebration of the novel *L'Été 1914*, the penultimate instalment of the suite known as *Les Thibault* by the French writer Roger Martin du Gard (1881–1958). First published in *Zeit und Welt. Gesammelte Aufsätze und Vorträge 1904–1940*, ed. Richard Friedenthal (Stockholm: Bermann-Fischer, 1943). Republished in *Zeiten und Schicksale. Aufsätze und Vorträge aus den Jahren 1902–1942*, ed. Knut Beck (Frankfurt: Fischer, 1990) [part of *Gesammelte Werke in Einzelbänden: Stefan Zweig*].

'THE SECRET OF ARTISTIC CREATION'
'Das Geheimnis des künstlerischen Schaffens' (1938)

Lecture given at a conference in London on 2nd December 1938, then in the United States during a reading tour of fifteen cities from 9th January to 14th February 1939. First published in *Zeit und Welt. Gesammelte Aufsätze und Vorträge 1904–1940*, ed. Richard Friedenthal (Stockholm: Bermann-Fischer, 1943). Republished in *Das Geheimnis des künstlerischen Schaffens: Essays*, ed. Knut Beck (Frankfurt: Fischer, 1984) [part of *Gesammelte Werke in Einzelbänden: Stefan Zweig*].

'THE HISTORIOGRAPHY OF TOMORROW'
'Geschichtsschreibung von morgen' (1939)

Lecture given during the US reading tour of January–February 1939. First published in *Zeit und Welt. Gesammelte Aufsätze und Vorträge 1904–1940*, ed. Richard Friedenthal (Stockholm: Bermann-Fischer, 1943), then later in *Die schlaflose Welt. Aufsätze und Vorträge aus den Jahren 1909–1941*, ed. Knut Beck (Frankfurt: Fischer, 1983) [part of *Gesammelte Werke in Einzelbänden: Stefan Zweig*].

'THE VIENNA OF YESTERDAY'
'Das Wien von gestern' (1940)

Lecture given in Paris at the Théâtre Marigny in April 1940. First published in *Zeit und Welt. Gesammelte Aufsätze und Vorträge 1904–1940*, ed. Richard Friedenthal (Stockholm: Bermann-Fischer, 1943). Republished in *Auf Reisen: Feuilletons und Berichte*, ed. Knut Beck (Frankfurt: Fischer, 1983) [part of *Gesammelte Werke in Einzelbänden: Stefan Zweig*].

'IN THIS DARK HOUR'
'In dieser dunklen Stunde' (1941)

Message of solidarity in the name of German writers in exile, presented at the banquet of the American PEN club in New York on 15th May 1941, on the occasion of the foundation of "European PEN in America". First published in *Aufbau*, a journal for German-speaking Jews, New York, 16th May 1941.

MORE FROM

STEFAN ZWEIG

HIS CLASSIC ELEGY FOR A EUROPE
DESTROYED BY TWO WORLD WARS

HIS ONLY FINISHED NOVEL –
TENSE, POWERFUL,
DEVASTATINGLY ACUTE.

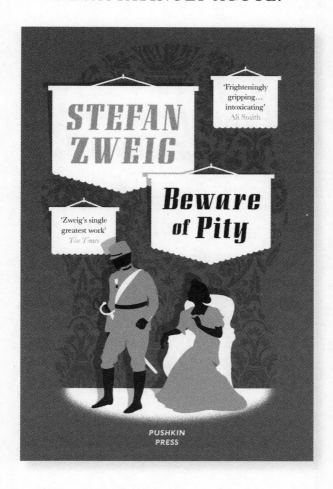

STEFAN ZWEIG

'A phenomenal, heartbreaking collection'
Los Angeles Review of Books

'Zweig belongs with those masters of the novella— Maupassant, Turgenev, Chekhov'
Paul Bailey

The Invisible Collection

Tales of Obsession and Desire

PUSHKIN
PRESS

TWO COLLECTIONS OF
HIS MOST SCINTILLATING
SHORT STORIES

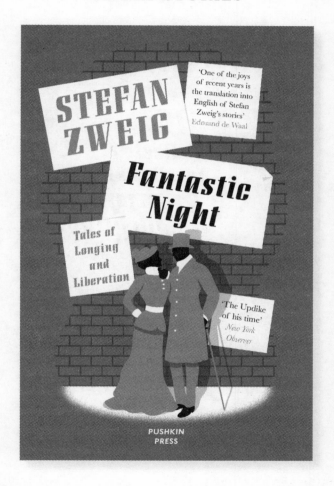

STEFAN
ZWEIG

'One of the joys
of recent years is
the translation into
English of Stefan
Zweig's stories'
Edmund de Waal

Fantastic
Night

Tales of
Longing
and
Liberation

'The Updike
of his time'
New York
Observer

PUSHKIN
PRESS

HIS MOST POWERFUL NOVELLAS

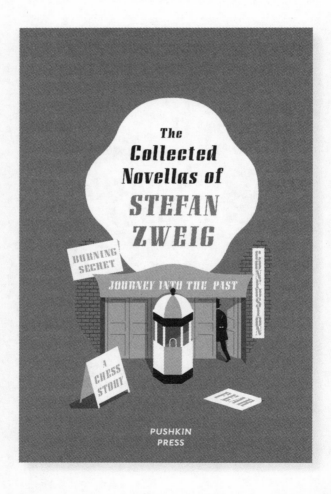

PUSHKIN PRESS

Pushkin Press was founded in 1997, and publishes novels, essays, memoirs, children's books—everything from timeless classics to the urgent and contemporary.

Our books represent exciting, high-quality writing from around the world: we publish some of the twentieth century's most widely acclaimed, brilliant authors such as Stefan Zweig, Marcel Aymé, Teffi, Antal Szerb, Gaito Gazdanov and Yasushi Inoue, as well as compelling and award-winning contemporary writers, including Andrés Neuman, Edith Pearlman, Eka Kurniawan and Ayelet Gundar-Goshen.

Pushkin Press publishes the world's best stories, to be read and read again. To discover more, visit www.pushkinpress.com.